TIPS FROM A MASTERMIND ON VARIOUS CAREER OPTIONS

A TRUE CAREER PATHFINDER
HOW TO CHOOSE A SUCCESSFUL CAREER?

INTERNATIONAL CIVIL SERVICES COMMISSION, UNITED NATIONS ORGANISATION, WORLD BANK, FORIEGN EDUCATION & MORE...

Dr. Tushaba Shinde, IRPS

BLUEROSE PUBLISHERS
India | U.K.

Copyright © Dr. Tushaba Shinde, IRPS 2024

All rights reserved by author. No part of this publication may be reproduced, stored in a retrieval system or transmitted in any form or by any means, electronic, mechanical, photocopying, recording or otherwise, without the prior permission of the author. Although every precaution has been taken to verify the accuracy of the information contained herein, the publisher assumes no responsibility for any errors or omissions. No liability is assumed for damages that may result from the use of information contained within.

BlueRose Publishers takes no responsibility for any damages, losses, or liabilities that may arise from the use or misuse of the information, products, or services provided in this publication.

For permissions requests or inquiries regarding this publication, please contact:

BLUEROSE PUBLISHERS
www.BlueRoseONE.com
info@bluerosepublishers.com
+91 8882 898 898
+4407342408967

ISBN: 978-93-6261-112-3

Book design, Cover design, Proofing, Re-editing and Digital freelancing by **Venkat**

Email : tushaba2000@yahoo.co.in
Email : assist.rvsquare@gmail.com

Phone : +91 93214 94877

Second Edition: October 2024

I dedicate this book to my beloved

Nana, my father,
Shri. Dashrathrao Shinde
Without him, I could not be with strong values and determination.

Aai, my mother,
Smt. Jayashiri Shinde
You are my strength, without you, I could have note been at this stage of life.

My wife,
Smt. Suvarna Shinde-Ogale
She is my love and inspiration for this book.

My loving brother,
Dear Prabhakar dada, Mahendra, Narendra & Ravindra;
And My loving daughters,
Anandita & Avantika
Very understanding, loving and motivated me to complete this book.

Acknowledgements

I am thankful to Mrs Neelam Chandra, IRSEE, Ex ADRM Pune who has guided and helped me in initial stage of book writing. She herself very renowned writer and author.

I am thankful to Mr Ganesh Shetty who is instrumental in this book writing and publication of first edition. No words to express gratitude for him. Also thankful to Mahendra, Harshada, Vishal for continuous support in book writing. Special thanks to Mrs Janhavi for kind help in this book. Thankful to Surya and Edwin for continuous support in this endeavour. Also, I would like to thank Mr. Venkat without whom it would have been difficult to publish the second edition of this book within time. He has worked hard and has continuously taken pain and efforts for this book.

WITH FOREWORD BY

Dr. Narendra Jadhav
Economist, Educationist and Author
Former Member of Parliament- Rajyasabha (Nominated)

In today's rapidly evolving world, the path to a successful and fulfilling career is more varied and complex than ever before. For young children dreaming of their future, young generation working in government and private sector but dreaming for good posts or international opportunities, for students considering higher education in India or abroad with scholarship, for social media career, for civil services career, the journey can be both exciting and daunting. This book aims to provide a comprehensive guide to 150 careers for helping each of these groups chart a clear course towards their goals.

Written by an experienced officer of the Indian Civil Service, this book offers insights and advice grounded in years of dedicated service and a deep understanding of the diverse opportunities available in modern careers. Whether you are a parent looking to guide your child, a student exploring a great career or foreign education options, or a professional in the present posting, this book is designed to support and inspire you.

For young children, the foundations of a successful career are built on curiosity, learning, and the nurturing of passions. This book provides parents with practical tips to encourage their children's interests and help them develop the skills and mindset needed for future success.

Ultimately, this book is a testament to the belief that with the right guidance and resources, anyone can achieve their career aspirations. The author, with his wealth of experience and knowledge, has crafted a guide that is both practical and inspiring. This book serves as a valuable resource for young minds and their mentors.

For professionals in private and government sectors, the book offers invaluable insights into career progression, effective job performance, and achieving a harmonious work-life balance. It recognizes the unique challenges faced by employees in these sectors and provides tailored strategies to navigate them.

I am deeply impressed by the breadth and depth of career guidance contained within these pages. The author has created a resource that is both practical and inspiring, grounded in his extensive experience and varied expertise.

I believe this book will serve as a beacon for all those who seek to navigate the complexities of the modern career landscape. It is a testament to the power of informed guidance and the limitless potential within each of us.

What is in this book?

       Basically, this book is especially written for all youngsters, parents and the ones who want to do best in their career, considering knowledge of all the fields in which they want to pursue their career.

Later, we have explained step by step, how to choose the best field for youngsters or themselves according to all scenarios. There should be no delay in choosing your field, if you really want to work hard and pursue a career as per one's best interest.

Author has given insight after each chapter and shared his experience of top people in every field with live examples. This will provide you a trigger to make a decision. You have to go through all the things explained, but at the end, you need to take a final call. Also web-link is given through which you can avail detailed information about a desired career field.

It discusses careers starting from 10th class to Graduation-Post

Graduation-Doctorate & Competitive exams where in many fields are inter-linked with each other. Ex-Candidates from Engineering with MBA are mostly preferred due to education background in various industries.

It also focusses on Foreign Education, International Career Opportunities in International Organisations like UNITED NATIONS, WORLD BANK, UNESCO etc.

Each career topic is illustrated through the best person in the field and explained what are career opportunities in the field. This ultimately motivates the youngsters and parents for future prospective.

Along with this, we have tried to bring the opinions of some of the best personalities from the field, which will resolve the doubts of the parents. Further we have sourced the information on various career topics linked with websites and institutions.

For the students who cannot pursue expensive courses or don't have any finances to study further, can get the help of scholarships which are mentioned thoroughly in the book. If anyone wants to opt for abroad studies, international career or some professional course, he can also get help from the various educational loans that are listed in the book, which are easy and economical.

This book is also written because there is a need for it. Many students are uncertain on How & What to choose for their career.

The book includes:
- The list of all the popular state, central and deemed universities which facilitates degree courses. It gives you a wide array to choose the best one from.
- The popular entrance exams that you can opt to pursue after passing 12th. (10+2)
- The professional courses which are highly paid and popular, these days.

- The valuable information on various scholarships at national and international level that are provided by the different organizations, that can help you finance your studies. There are students who are unaware about these scholarships and at times the deserving students also miss out on due to lack of information. This book keeps you well-informed about it.
- The details of the various economic educational loans provided by various banks. The list of these banks is provided.
- The crucial information about the requirements to study abroad is also included for the students who aspire to study in other countries. These details include the best countries to study abroad after 12th, the top courses they provide and the types of visas offered by the governments of these countries. We tried to provide how GRE/other exams can be cracked to get admission in universities successfully. Also, how to get guidance for finance and how to approach the university.
- Most important part to know about what are the different avenues available in international organization/position.

Also, how to enquire, how to approach, what is the required qualification, criteria etc are given here. Problem is that people do not know about these opportunities which can be easily availed by everyone.

The Author's aim is to provide all information about courses, institutions, their websites to you with a theoretical framework, the expected results and with a step-by-step process of career guidance which could be easily implemented in your life.

Hope this book definitely helps & facilitates students to choose their right career paths.

Wishing you all **BEST OF LUCK** for the journey towards a bright and successful career and one day will love to see you all at the pinnacle of success.

About the Author

Dr. Tushaba Shinde is from Parbhani district, Marathwada region of Maharashtra state. He took education from regional marathi medium school and came from a middle-class family. During his junior college days of 11th standard, he learned about Mr. Kofi Annan, SECRETARY GENERAL of UNITED NATIONS through newspaper which was available in the Municipal Council Library at Parbhani. This was a great inspiration wherein Mr. Annan was in charge of the whole World as Head of UNO. Under this banner, he could help poor people and help war affected areas through peace keeping forces.

This moment was of great motivation for little Tushaba and he started to search how to get into UNO. Then he learned about INDIAN FOREIGN SERVICE (IFS) through competitive magazines. That moment, he decided to appear in CIVIL SERVICES EXAM and become IFS.

This time frame started the journey of UPSC. He started taking more efforts to gain knowledge. Library became his temple and this is the place where he used to sleep at night from 7th class till 12th class.

After 12th class, he scored 90 percentile in Medical PCB. Till 1998 in Maharashtra, admission to medical colleges used to be on the basis of aggregate marks of 3 subjects like PCB (PHYSICS, CHEMISTRY AND BIOLOGY).

On this basis, he got an admission in BDS and BAMS. He chose BAMS, as college was in Mumbai where he can study UPSC in a better way. The SIAC (State Administrative Career Institute, Mumbai) is a government sponsored UPSC Training Institute accompanied him for his study.

During medical college years, he was not able to speak a single sentence grammatically correct. That too he understood when he wrote an essay for UPSC during second year and showed it to one of his colleagues. Then he took help from friends who were from convent medium. That was the time when he started to speak with friends in English even with professors and the dean of medical college. Most of the colleagues used to laugh but he never felt bad. But many of them supported him, like DEAN of the college MR. KOHLI appreciated him in front of journalist and said one day this guy will do big thing.

He started preparation for UPSC but he was not having enough money. Hence, he started doing a job in a corporate company. But he could not clear the exam. Later he decided to go to DELHI and prepare it with full commitment. But he was not having financial support from anyone.

Due to this, he joined Assistant Commandant Post as he cleared this exam earlier. This exam is also conducted by UPSC. At that time, he got to make a friend MR. PRAMOD PAWAR from Ahmednagar who was at Assistant Commandant Training Centre - Gurgaon, Haryana. He just listened to his problem and assured that he will provide support to Tushaba for continuing his study.

He gave financial support during this period and for which Tushaba is indebted for his friendship and their bond of affection still continues.

Dr. Tushaba understood one thing on that day, if you have will, then everything supports you to get your goal. But you must do your hard work consistently. Definitely God will always support you. Then, he never turned back.

The Dean sir's words came true and he got selected through UPSC and he was the first student from Podar Medical college to crack the exam. Best part of this is that he got the highest mark in the Civil Services Exam Interview within the students from Maharashtra state. This was a great achievement for him especially when he was not able to speak English properly. After that other student from medical college also started preparing for UPSC, MPSC, MBA and other corporate jobs. He broke the ice first and others started to follow it.

Most important thing is to tell you why this book is being written. Because, when he started preparation for UPSC and got selected through it. Later he understood that How to get into UNO. There is a separate examination called YOUNG PROFESSIONAL PROGRAMME (YPP). It is a separate exam conducted by UNO like our Civil Services Examination in India. They recruit yearly from specific countries especially who do not get representation. Also, they prefer women's representation as they are under-represented.

Dr. Tushaba Shinde needed the guidance which he could not get, and he learned that the similar problem should not be faced by other aspirants. Also, there are great opportunities in international organizations, various masters, doctoral programs offered by top 100 universities in the world based on GRE score and scholarship etc. This information is not available to all candidates. This book is for those who want to know various opportunities in variety of fields in India and abroad. This book also illustrates various options like social media career, IT field, various exams etc which our people do not know. Once they know, they will come with flying colours. Only they need to get proper guidance.

He is now heading the Human Resource Department of Mumbai Division of Central Railway. He looks after the HR of all departments like operations, commercial, mechanical etc. Under this, he looks after promotion, transfer, training, settlement and also the matters of pensioners. Overall, he is incharge of HR activities for 45,000 staff and pensioners.

He has worked in Pune Division,

Nanded Division, Bhusaval Division and also worked in South Central Railway (SCR) Head Quarter at Secunderbad. At SCR HQ, he was in charge of welfare of 1.23 Lakh employees. It was a great experience wherein he was looking after the welfare of all staff and their families.

Also, he is more focused on the digitalization of Human Resource Activities. This is the reason when he was in charge of personnel department at Bhusaval Division, he was recognised for 12 consecutively 4 times for the award of **'PERSONNEL SHIELD'** as Best Personnel Department.

With this, presently he developed a complete package of digital personnel department and uploaded it through www.railkarmikseva.com. Here all work of HR is digitalized and 100% work is being done through e-office. Under his leadership, the HRMS (Human Resource Management System) package is developed and the whole department is now working on it. Now all staff can also work from home. In short corporate culture is developed under his leadership in government organization. This is also appreciated by MEMBER SECRETARY and PCPO/CR.

He also wished to guide those who want to go abroad for higher studies and those who want to make a career in international organization. Presently he is doing Ph.D.in Labour Economics from Gokhale Institute of Politics & Economics, Pune.

What is required to be successful in your career?

There is not a single thing or single formula which is fit for success. There is a combination of things required for successful life and career.

These are as follows:
First and most important thing is PASSION for doing something like acting, wanting to achieve a goal, getting a lot of money. This motivates people and helps people to do work in the long term without break and tiredness. Doing work is not important but doing it for long term with consistent zeal with the best input is necessary.

> *"Without Passion, Nothing will Happen!*
> *More You are Passionate about Your Goal,*
> *More You will be Successful..."*
> *- Dr. Tushaba Shinde, IRPS*

Second thing is that no career is bad or good like doctor, engineer, business, social-work or cleaning road etc. You can make a successful career in any of the above, but you need to do it with full commitment, dedication and passion. You may ask how it is possible to compare all above at one platform. This can be explained by putting in simple words like every person has different likes and wants to do something new in different fields.

One may become successful in becoming a doctor and earn good money, whereas one can become successful by sweeping. One may ask, how one becomes successful in sweeping, why not? He can do the business of sweeping roads through contracts and earn in crores which is much higher than any other profession like doctor or engineer. Through this we can understand that it is not necessary to have only talent to be successful but hard work also pays.

Third is, earlier you understand your GOAL; chances of being successful is more for you. This is due to mastery over it through continuous efforts. Like doing efforts on arts, sports or IAS Preparation rather than doing preparation in the latter stage.

You may see that those who have earlier background in any field have a very high success ratio. For example, in China, based on natural talent, the government chose candidates at an early age in which they should make a career like running, boxing according to their natural capacity and to prepare for international competition. To achieve a financial goal it is said that, earlier you start saving, your growth of money will be higher. Same way, earlier you understand the goal, you achieve it early without any problem.

> *"Earlier You Start Preparing for Your Goal,*
> *The Chances of Achieving the Goal Earlier is More.*
> *Hence, Always Start Preparing for a Goal in an Early Stage."*
> *- Dr. Tushaba Shinde, IRPS*

Fourth, you need to FOCUS on only one thing rather than many things during career preparation. By doing many things at one moment, you may lose sight and get failure due to loss of energy in many areas. Hence our target, ambition and goal should be only in one direction in any condition. Otherwise, chances of failure would increase. Sometimes you know this, but fail to implement it.

Fifth, a person should always DREAM BIG which is basic for achieving bigger goals. SWAMI VIVEKANANDA always used to say that a person should see such dreams which never allow a person to sleep peacefully. That is a real dream. Then only a person can achieve the goal with rigorous efforts.

Parents should allow children what they want to do in their life. They should never force their ambition on their head which never succeeds in their life or their parent's life. **THREE IDIOT MOVIE** is a great example of life and each one should follow. Many times, people understand it but could not apply it to their life.

Parents should not give anything easily to their children and fulfil their demands & wishes. Instead, they should imply N-1 theory in which some demands should be kept unfulfilled. This is a very important thing for children in today's world. This is due to easy money for children and they get over pampered. Due to this, they become more adamant and possessive. They never try to adjust with public life. Hence every parent should focus and have huge responsibility in all respects of children as well as their family. Children are like mud; they get shape as you give them. You are responsible for developing them or destroying them. This is bluntly adding to increasing tendency of suicide by students.

This happens due to over focusing on study and bothering children to become a Doctor or Engineer. Person can make a career in any field and can live life successfully with dignity.
Even MR. RATAN TATA used to say that life is much beyond success, money but real success lies with health, wealth and family. Even if one is missing from above one can destroy one's purpose in life.

"When you want to become smart and learn something extra, then always be with smarter people than you, and have an interaction with these people.

You will observe that you are in the success bracket."
- Dr. Tushaba Shinde, IRPS

There are three things required in life:

KNOWLEDGE, INTELLIGENCE, AND HARDWORK.

The first two things will make a difference in success. But without hard work, earlier two will be useless. Hence Hard Work is the most important among all.

- Dr. Tushaba Shinde, IRPS

CONTENTS

Best Courses after 10th Standard....16
- *Industrial Training Institute Courses........16*
- *Diploma in Engineering....17*
- *Medical Courses After 10th Standard...17*
- *Opportunity in Indian Armed Forces.....18*

Best Courses after 12th Standard (10+2) 20
- *Choosing Engineering as a Career....21*
- *Degree Courses in Commerce....24*
- *Courses in Arts & Humanities.....25*
- *Diploma Courses after 12th Science.....25*
- *Career Scope in Science Stream.....26*
- *Various Engineering Options....27*
- *Robotics.....46*
- *Textile Engineering....47*
- *Agricultural Science....48*
- *Bio-Technology....49*
- *Computer Applications.....49*
- *Computer Science.....50*
- *Cyber Security.....51*
- *Earth Science / Geography....51*
- *Environmental Science....52*
- *Food Technology....53*
- *Forestry....54*
- *Oceanography....55*
- *Mathematics & Statistical Science.....55*
- *Wildlife Biology....56*
- *MBBS....57*
- *Ayurveda – BAMS....57*
- *Dental – BDS....58*
- *Homeopathy – BHMS....59*
- *Naturopathy....59*
- *Pharmacy....60*
- *Siddha....61*
- *Unani....62*
- *Anthropology....62*
- *Archaeology & Art Restoration....63*
- *Educational Counselor....64*
- *Monuments & Sculpture Restoration....64*
- *Museology....66*
- *Physiotherapy....66*
- *Social Work....67*
- *LAW....68*
- *Advertising....69*

- Media, Mass Communication & Journalism....**69**
- Public Relations.....**71**
- Art Direction....**71**
- Choreography....**72**
- Direction.....**72**
- Film & Drama.....**73**

Performing Arts.....74
- Vocal & Instrumental.....**74**
- Visual Art, Communication & Animation.....**75**
- Cinematography.....**75**
- Communication Design.....**76**
- Design.....**77**
- Graphic Designing....**77**
- Photography.....**78**
- Actuarial Science.....**78**
- Bank Management.....**79**
- Business Administration.....**79**
- Chartered Accountancy....**80**
- Certified Financial Advisor – CFA.....**81**
- Event Management.....**82**
- Hospital Management.....**83**
- Hotel Management.....**83**
- Human Resource Management.....**84**
- Insurance.....**85**
- Bachelor of Education - B.Ed.....**86**
- Corporate Intelligence – Detective.....**86**
- Interior Designing.....**87**
- Library Science....**88**
- Nutrition & Dietetics.....**88**
- Career in Politics....**89**
- Research Scientist.....**89**

Interesting Career for Interesting Students....90
- Alcohol Technology....**90**
- Astro-Biology....**91**
- Fishery....**92**
- Food Flavorist / Food Chemist....**93**
- Gardening Programme....**94**
- Mountaineering....**94**
- Pet Grooming....**95**
- Public Health Entomology....**95**
- SPA Management.....**96**
- Tea Tasting.....**197**
- Excellent Career Ideas for Language Learners....**98**

- *Do You Want a Career in Foreign Language....**99***
- *Which Foreign Language to Learn in India....**100***
- *Travel & Tourism....**102***
- *Sports & Sports Management....**102***
- *Sports & Physical Education....**103***
- *Career in Super Sports....**104***
- *Indian Railway Service.....**106***
- *Social Media Career.....**108***
- *Toughest Exams in the World....**111***
- *UPSC-Civil Service Examination....**113***
- *IAS Preparation Tips for Beginners....**116***
- *Indian Engineering Services Exam....**120***
- *Indian Forest Service Exam.....**121***
- *Central Armed Police Forces.....**123***
- *National Defense Academy & Naval Academy....**125***
- *State Public Service Examination....**127***
- *Foreign Education....**129***
- *National Overseas Scholarship Scheme....**131***
- *Graduate Record Examination (GRE) **134***
- *Scholastic Assessment Test (SAT)....**135***
- *Common Admission Test (CAT) **136***
- *Post-Doctoral Research & Scientific Career....**137***
- *International Career - UNITED NATIONS & Others.....**139***
- *International Civil Service Commission-ICSC....**141***
- *Young Professional Programme (YPP)....**149***
- *Bank Loans for Education.....**150***
- *Free Education Website....**151***
- *International Opportunities.....**153***
- *How to consistently be successful and wealthy? **154***
- *Interviews of Renowned Personalities....**158***

BEST COURSES AFTER 10TH STANDARD

These are vast career opportunities after 10th standard which parents should know where children can have a great career. This may sound odd but this is true provided the child should take interest and do great work in that field. I will explain step by step.

The list I am providing is based on various facts. Firstly, I am considering the cost involved in any best course after 10th standard. Secondly, I am including those courses available through-out India. So even if you are living in a village or semi-rural area, it would be easy to find a course near home.

INDUSTRIAL TRAINING INSTITUTE COURSES

The vocational courses available from Industrial Training Institutes (ITI) is the best option after 10th standard.

ITI courses are recognized by every industry. Also, ITI has some of the best courses after 10th standard that will enable you to find excellent jobs. ITI courses will give you a Diploma Certificate.

Here are the best courses after 10th standard from ITI:

Agricultural Farm Management	Air Conditioning & Refrigeration Technician	Airline Steward/Stewards
Automobile Electrical Technician	Automobile Mechanical Technician	Baking & Confectioning
Body & Beauty Care	Caregiver	Chemical Plant Operator
Civil Draftsman	Communications Equipment Technician	Corporate Housekeeping
Dairy Management	Data Entry Operator	Dental Lab Technician
Denture Maker	Desktop Publishing	Event Management
Facilities Management (Old-age homes, Hospitals, etc)	Fashion Designing	Fireman and Disaster Relief
Floriculture & Commercial Landscaping	Food Processing	Food Technician

Horticultural	Hospital Staff	IT and Electronic Management
Laboratory Technician	Legal/ Para-Legal Assistant	Logistics Assistant
Mechanical Draftsman	Medical Technician	Nutrition Assistant
Photography	Quantity Surveyor	Welding Technician

The good news is that ITI courses are available for women and men of any age. Infact, a lot of new courses are now offered by ITI and also offered by private institutes to recruit them in companies directly. Also, it is geared through the Skills India Program of the Indian Government, wherein you can get courses at low cost.

For more information on courses after 10th Standard you may visit below listed websites:
https://www.aplustopper.com/iti-courses/
https://study.com/articles/Mechanical_Drafter_Career_Information_and_Requirements_for_Becoming_a_Mechanical_Drafter.html

DIPLOMA IN ENGINEERING

You may also consider doing a Diploma in Engineering from any reputed polytechnic in India. It is also one of the best courses after 10th standard.

Diploma in Engineering is available in the following streams:

- Chemical Engineering
- Civil Engineering
- Electrical Engineering
- Mechanical Engineering
- Metallurgical Engineering

MEDICAL COURSES AFTER 10th STANDARD

You can opt for paramedical courses after 10th class and get a good job. Also, you become an independent earner in the family.

- Diploma in Rural Healthcare
- Diploma in Hospital Assistance
- Diploma in Nursing Assistance
- Diploma in Paramedic Nursing

Pathology Lab Technician

India is becoming a world leader and promoting itself as a world-class medical tourism destination. Also, there are several new hospitals and healthcare facilities that are opening across the country.

IT & COMPUTER TECHNOLOGY

This is a very good option in the IT Industry of India where you have great opportunities after 10th standard. Later completion of these listed courses, you can take admission in the Degree course of Computer in Engineering College.

Certificate in Search Engine Marketing

Certificate in Search Engine Optimization

Certificate in Social Media Management

Diploma in Computer Technician

OPPORTUNITY IN INDIAN ARMED FORCES

This is one of the best career options after 10th class. It is one of the favorite options for youngsters from some areas of India who have Army background in Family.

Solider (General Duty)

Solider (Tradesman)

Regardless of which course you opt, it is compulsory to serve the Indian Armed Forces upon completion of training. There are various options according to trade available in **INDIAN ARMY**.

> *"Army is the True Nobility of our Country"*
> *- Napolean Bonaparte*

Final Thoughts:
Millions of students opt for these courses after 10th Standard due to many reasons, mainly due to financial reasons. However, it does not mean that life ends here. If a person has strong passion and desire to do hard work and have a goal, then sky is limit for them. One can

do anything in his life provided he should do efforts in the right direction.

How to choose 12th Class Streams:

It is observed that many students are confused after 10th class due to various reasons. i.e.:

- Students have not decided what would be their career goal
- Students may not know what to do
- Lack of guidance to students by parents
- Students simply studying without having any goal in their mind
- Family is not serious about the career of a child
- In India, there is no awareness among parents

BEST COURSES AFTER 12TH STANDARD (10+2)

This is a life changing juncture where students take move to their respective fields. Afterwards, their goal changes and their academic life becomes more meaningful. If students are confident and determined for their goal, more are the chances to achieve the goal.

There is a bright future for science students due to more opportunities for them. They can move from science to commerce or arts field but other two fields cannot opt science field directly. There are many fields like biology (life sciences) or mathematics which can be combined or opted separately. Afterwards anyone can opt specialization in one of the fields according to the wish of the candidate.

COURSES AFTER 12TH WITH PCB

Following are the options who have biology background as follows:

B.Sc.	B.Sc. Dairy Technology	B.Sc. Home Science
B.Sc. Nursing	Bachelor of Naturopathy & Yogic Science	Bachelor of Veterinary Science & Animal Husbandry
Bachelor of Pharmacy	BAMS (Ayurvedic)	BDS
BHMS (Homeopathy)	Biotechnology	BMLT (Medical Lab Technology)
BOT (Occupational Therapy)	BUMS (Unani)	General Nursing
Integrated M.Sc.	MBBS	Paramedical Courses

For more information on courses after 12th Science with PCB you may visit the below website:
https://www.sarvgyan.com/courses/science-courses

COURSES AFTER 12TH WITH PCM

Students with PCM group in 12th standard can pursue their further study in engineering & technology, pharmacy, architecture, law, management, fashion, textile, social work, library science etc.

B. Arch	B.A	B.CA
B. Com	B.Sc	C.A Program
C.S Program	Competitive Exams UPSC	Defense (Army, Navy, Air Force)
Designing Courses	Education/ Teaching	Engineering (B.E/B.Tech)
Environmental Science	Fashion Technology	Film & Television Courses
Foreign Education	Hospitality Management	Hotel Management
ICWA Program	IIT	LLB (Bachelor of Law)
M. Tech.	Media/ Journalism Courses	PhD Programme in various fields
Social Worker	State Public Service Commission Exams	Travel & Tourism Courses
UDCT MUMBAI		

For more information on courses after 12th Science with PCM you may visit the below website:
http://www.mapmytalent.in/courses-after-12th

CHOOSING ENGINEERING AS A CAREER

Engineering is one of the most demanding career areas in the education sector which is in demand by most of the industries. Following are degree courses available to opt from.

B. Tech/Bachelor of Engineering in Civil Engg	B. Tech /Bachelor of Engineering in Computer Science	B. Tech /Bachelor of Engineering in Dairy Technology
B. Tech /Bachelor of Engineering in Electrical	B. Tech /Bachelor of Engineering in Electronics & Tele-communication	B. Tech /Bachelor of Engineering in Information Technology
B. Tech /Bachelor of Engineering in Mechanical		

Other specializations include marine, aerospace, agricultural, Petroleum, Automobile, Biochemical, Bio Medical, Biotechnology, Bio Instrumentation, Bioinformatics, Chemical, Environmental, Food technology, Fire, Leather, Mining & Metallurgical, Nano-technology, Printing, Plastic & polymer, Rubber, Genetic, Textile etc.

Eligibility: 12th Science PCM with high percentile.

Admission procedure: Now national level exams are conducted. Whereas some states give admission based on 12th standard marks or state level entrance exams. National Level entrance test such as IIT-JEE, GATE, UPSEE, BITSAT are also conducted.

CAREER IN MERCHANT NAVY

This is one of the lucrative career options for those who dream of a challenging and adventurous career. It comprises below courses which require a good amount of undergoing rigorous training curriculum.

Bachelor of Science in Nautical Technology (3 years training at Institute + 1 year at Sea).

Bachelor of Technology in Naval Architecture and Ship Building

Higher National Diploma (HND) Nautical Science or Marine Engineering (1 year course)

Eligibility: 12th Science PCM with high percentile.

Admission procedure: The All-India Merchant Navy Entrance Test (AIMNET), required the good vision (eyesight) and perfect health standards.

CAREER AS A COMMERCIAL PILOT

As the world has come closer due to Aviation and drastic use of new evolving technology, commercial pilots are in demand globally. Choosing a career as a Commercial Pilot one needs to qualify the below courses:

Commercial Pilot Training Programme from Aviation Institutes in India

B.Sc in Aviation Sciences

Eligibility: 12th Science PCM with high percentile.

Admission procedure: Admission is based on an All-India Written Test, Pilot Aptitude Test (WOMBAT) and an interview. Required good eyesight and health.

BACHELOR OF SCIENCE

One may opt for a bachelor's degree in Science and it has various options to continue and later pursue Masters in a particular subject. Below are the options one can opt for:

Physics, Chemistry, Maths, Astronomy, Forensic Science, Geology, Statistics, Industrial Chemistry, Nautical Science, Home Science, Nutrition, Clothing and Textile, Extension and Communication, Environmental Science, Human Development and Family Studies, Fashion Design, Fashion Technology etc.

Eligibility: 12th Science PCM with minimum 55% percentile.

Admission procedure: Merit based admission; few institutes conduct entrance exam.

NATIONAL DEFENSE SERVICES

The National Defense Academy, Pune (NDA) offers only a full-time, residential undergraduate program. Cadets are awarded a bachelor's degree (a Bachelor of Arts or a Bachelor of Science or a Bachelor of Technology) after 3 years of study. Cadets have a choice of two streams of study. The Science stream offers studies in Physics, Chemistry, Mathematics and Computer Science. The Humanities (Liberal Arts) stream offers studies in History, Economics, Political Science, Geography and Language.

Eligibility: 12th PCM, unmarried Indian citizens.

Admission procedure: National level NDA Entrance Exam.

RAILWAY APPRENTICE EXAM

Indian Railways is one of the biggest recruiters in India. An Apprentice Programme is offered by the organization to nurture the new upcoming talent in the country. The selected candidates get trained for four years, not just in the field of mechanical and electrical engineering; they are also groomed to take up leadership positions in the Indian Railways as Class 1 officers.

Eligibility: 12th Science PCM with first class

Admission procedure: All India Special Railway Apprentice Exam by UPSC.

BUSINESS ADMINISTRATION & MANAGEMENT STUDIES

In order to keep pace with the changing industries and management styles in corporate culture, listed degree courses are eminent.

Bachelor of Business Administration (BBA)
Bachelor of Management Studies (BMS)

Eligibility: 12th Science, Commerce or Arts with 55% & above

Admission procedure: Entrance Test or by Merit.

DEGREE COURSES IN COMMERCE

Due to a growing economy and upcoming new ventures, the commerce stream is considered as a backbone of a country. This sector has opened doors for some good career options.

Bachelor of Commerce (B. Com)   *Banking & Insurance (BBI)*
Chartered Accountancy (CA)

Eligibility: 12th Science or Commerce with 55% & above

Admission procedure: Admission for B.Com is based on merit and CA/CS has National Level Exam.

COURSES IN ARTS & HUMANITIES

Bachelor of Arts (Physcology, Sociology, Foreign Languages, Travel, Tourism, English & Archaeology)

Bachelor in Physical Education (BPE)

Bachelor in Social Work (BSW)

Mass Communication & Journalism

Eligibility: 12th Science/Commerce with 55% & above

Admission procedure: Admission to BA courses is based on merit and admission for other mentioned courses is based on entrance exam or an interview.

DIPLOMA COURSES AFTER 12th SCIENCE

Air Crew	Air Hostess	Animation & Multimedia
Animation Film Making	Application Software Development (DASD)	Arts & A/V Editing
Bachelor in Beauty Culture & Hair Dressing	Computer Courses	Cutting & Tailoring
Drawing & Painting	Dress Designing (DDD)	Event Management
Fashion Designing (DFD)	Film Computer Hardware	Film Making & Digital Video Production
Foreign Language Courses	Graphic Designing	Hospital & Health Care Management
HR Training	Information Technology	Mass Communication
Mass Media & Creative Writing	Physical Medicine & Rehabilitation	Print Media Journalism & Communication
Textile Designing	Web Designing	

For more information on various courses after 12th Standard you may visit the website below:
https://www.collegedekho.com/articles/diploma-courses-after-class-12-science-duration-job-and-salary-scope/

CAREER SCOPE IN SCIENCE STREAM

There are many career options available for 12th science students after passing out. The best part of science stream is that students can switch to other careers i.e. arts, humanities or even to commerce. To build a great career, you must need at least a graduation degree. After earning a bachelor's degree, you can find employment in any sector. Once you have completed your graduation, you will have a wide range of job opportunities.

You have many options as follows:
You can be a healthcare professional, engineer, creator, business professional scientist, or a teacher/professor, etc.

Still not satisfied, want to learn more, read on:
This is one of the most confusing periods in the students' life. First you should counsel yourself. Suppose that;

You have chosen PCM group or PCB group or Commerce or Arts in 12th standard. It means you have chosen your area of interest. Do not be surprised or tense. You have done your best.

But yes, off course, if you wish to change your field for higher studies, you can go through many options according to your interest.

Anyone having Art stream in 12th standard can pursue his further study in art, humanities, management, media, fashion, journalism or tourism.

If a student is having PCM or Maths in 12th standard can pursue his further study in engineering & technology, pharmacy, architecture, and all art group fields. Also, the students from any of the above streams can pursue their further studies in law, management, fashion, textile, social work and library science.

For more information you may visit the website below:
https://www.sarvgyan.com/courses/science-coursehttps://www.iaspaper.net/courses-after-12th-science/

AERONAUTICAL ENGINEERING

This sector mainly focuses on the design, production testing and maintenance of aircrafts in defense and commercial areas. It is growing fast and has a great future. It has advanced education in developed nations. Exceptional country like India only has expertise in this field.

Eligibility: 12th Science with PCB
Post Graduate Level: Under-Graduate Engineering degree in Aeronautical or Aerospace.
Doctoral Level: Post-Graduate Engineering degree in Aeronautical or Aerospace.

Courses:

B.Tech & B. in Aeronautical Engineering

M.E. in Aeronautical Engineering

M.Tech & M.E in Avionics

M.Tech in Aeronautical Engineering

Ph.D

Institutes & Universities:

Institute of Aeronautical Engineering, Hyderabad

Amity University, Mumbai

CM Engineering College, Hyderabad

Abroad Education:

University of Texas, Austin, USA

MIT

Salary:

The average salary for an Aerospace/ Aeronautical Engineer in India ranges between INR. 35,000 to INR.1lakh per month. The maximum salary offered to an Aerospace/ Aeronautical Engineer graduated from IITs is INR 30 lakhs per annum (in software field).

AERONAUTICAL ENGINEERING

This is one of the very interesting fields where everyone is fascinated by curiosity. It focuses on research, design, development and manufacturing of spacecraft and aircraft. It has two branches like aeronautical engineering which deals with earth's atmosphere and astronautical engineering which deals with outside earth's atmosphere.

Eligibility: 12th Science with PCB

Under Graduate Level: 10+2 /12th with Physics, Chemistry &Maths and need to qualify in JEE

Post Graduate Level: Under-Graduate Engineering degree in Aeronautical or Aerospace or related Engineering or both

Doctoral Level: Must have completed Post-Graduation in Aeronautical / Aerospace Engineering & valid GATE score

Courses:

B.Tech in Aerospace Engineering   M.Tech in Aerospace Engineering

Ph.D

Institutes & Universities:

IIT - Mumbai, Madras, Chennai

Salary:
The average basic Aerospace Engineering job salary in India per year ranges from 15Lakhs to 20Lakhs, anything between INR. 4Lakhs to 6Lakhs, the salary increases gradually with experience.

For more information you may visit the website below:
www.amecet.co
https://www.iist.ac.in/admissions/undergraduate/btech-aerospace-engineering
https://www.aero.iitb.ac.in/home/

*"**Avul Pakir Jainulabdeen Abdul Kamal:** A Famous Personality who really made it Big in the world of Aerospace Engineering"*

ARCHITECTURE ENGINEERING

This sector deals with the construction of buildings with planning, designing, safety of buildings. Also includes innovative ideas regarding new structures with difference. It has a great future if one has new ideas and ability to do hard work.

Eligibility: 10+2 /12th with PCM and JEE

Courses:

B. Arch   M. Arch

Ph.D

Institutes & Universities:

IIT - Mumbai, Kharagpur, Roorkee, Delhi   College of Engineering, Pune

BHU, Varanasi

Salary:

While a beginner can expect to earn anything between INR. 4Lakhs to 6Lakhs per annum, the salary increases gradually with experience.

*"**Leonardo di ser Piero da Vinci:** A Famous Personality who really made it Big in the world of Architecture Engineering"*

ARTIFICIAL INTELLIGENCE & MACHINE LEARNING

Artificial Intelligence focuses on the development of highly developed computers and machines which work like humans with brain. This includes speech recognition, visual perception, logic and decision making, multi-language translation, work in spy activities and where humans cannot work.

Eligibility: 10+2 /12th Science

Courses:

B. Tech   M. Tech

Ph.D

Institutes & Universities:

IISc - Bangalore, Bombay, Kharagpur   IIIT- Hyderabad, Allahabad

IIT, Madras

Salary:
The average salary for a Data Scientist, IT with Machine Learning skills is INR. 8Lakhs per year. Entry-level Artificial Intelligence salary in India for almost 40% of professionals earn around INR. 6,00,000, mid-level and senior-level artificial intelligence salary could earn more than INR. 50,00,000 in India.

For more information you may visit the website below:
https://pathmind.com/wiki/ai-vs-machine-learning-vs-deep-learning

ASTRONOMY & ASTROPHYSICS

It deals with study of celestial bodies in space. Also, it measures calculation of orbits, gravitational forces, galaxies, other space related objects which are useful for study. Astrophysics is a branch of Astronomy. It deals with detailed study of the physical, chemical and dynamic properties of celestial objects. It is very fascinating for children in early years.

Eligibility: 10+2 /12th with PCM

Courses:

M.Sc. Astronomy M.Sc. Astrophysics

Ph.D

Institutes & Universities:

University of Mumbai, Mumbai

Indian Institute of Astrophysics, Bangalore

Indian Institute of Science, Bangalore

Inter-University Centre for Astronomy & Astrophysics (IUCAA)-Pune

National Centre for Radio Astronomy, Pune

Tata Fundamental Research Institute, Pune

Aryabhatta Research Institute of Observational Science (ARIES)-Nainital

Salary:

Astronomers usually earn a PhD degree in Physics, Astronomy or Astrophysics. Astronomers on an average earn INR. 8Lakhs to INR. 10Lakhs annually.

For more information you may visit the website below:

https://www.aanda.org/

https://career.webindia123.com/career/institutes/list_colleges_Institutes.asp?group=129

"**Aryabhatta**: A Famous Personality who really made it Big in the world of Mathematics and Astronomy"

AUTOMOBILE ENGINEERING

It is focused to develop, design, fabricate, and test vehicles or vehicle components from the concept stage to manufacturing stage by incorporating various elements of engineering.

Eligibility: 10+2 /12th with PCM and JEE for IIT
Courses:

B. Tech   M. Tech

Ph.D

Institutes & Universities:

BHU, Varanasi   College of Engineering, Pune

Maulana Abdul Kalam Azad University of Technology, West - Bengal

Salary:
In India, the average salary of an Automotive Engineer is ranging from INR. 3Lakhs to INR. 6Lakhs per annum (as a fresher). And an experienced Automotive Engineer with a master's degree can earn more than INR. 10Lakhs per annum.
For more information you may visit the website below:
https://www.shiksha.com/engineering/automobile-engineering-chp

*"**Henry Ford:** A Famous Personality who really made it Big in the world of Automobile Engineering"*

BIOMEDICAL ENGINEERING

It is related to application of engineering knowledge to the medical field which helps in formulation of new drugs, new medical diagnostic machinery, patient instruments, rehabilitation equipment, etc. Professionals in this field are known as a biomedical engineer. The biomedical engineers utilize the engineering methods and theories to enhance health care. Also, it involves tissue culture technology for drug formulation, techniques for the benefit of the medical field.

Eligibility: 10+2 /12th with Biology

Courses:

B. Sc	B. Tech in Biomedical Engineering
M.Tech	Ph.D

Institutes & Universities:

All India Institute of Medical Sciences, New Delhi

Dr. B.R. Ambedkar Centre of Biomedical Research, University of Delhi

Salary:
Biomedical Engineer's median salary is around INR. 6 to 8Lakhs per annum.
For more information you may visit the website below:
https://collegedunia.com/courses/bachelor-of-technology-btech-biomedical-engineering
https://topyaps.com/top-10-colleges-in-india-for-biomedical-engineering/

BIOTECHNOLOGY ENGINEERING

It deals with research in genetics, molecular technology, tissue culture, microbiology, animal husbandry, vaccine formulation, drug formulation and healing of patients. It involves branches like genetics, biochemistry, microbiology, etc. It includes various things like Gene therapy, Immune technologies, Genetic Engineering, Drug Design, Stem cell techniques, New DNA technologies, Photosynthetic efficiency, Enzyme Engineering and technology.

Future Prospects: It has very great prospects in the future due to advanced technology in the area of medicine, industry, agriculture and its production, development of new food species, drug efficiency etc. Due to this, there would be intense demand for these graduates in future.

Eligibility: 10+2 /12th with PCB /Biology

Courses:

Bachelor of Engineering in Biotechnology

Bachelor of Technology in Bioprocess Technology & Engineering

M.Tech

Ph.D

Institutes & Universities:

IIT- Mumbai, Chennai, Delhi

Salary:
Biotechnologist Job Salary in India is with an average salary of INR. 5-7Lakhs per year.
For more information you may visit the website below:
https://university.careers360.com/colleges/list-of-biotechnology-universities-in-india

*"**Mr. C V Raman:** A Famous Personality who really made it Big in the world of Biotechnology Engineering"*

CERAMICS ENGINEERING

These are heat resistant materials which are used in industries like mining, aerospace, medicine, refinery, food and chemical industries, electronics, signal and telecommunication industries, and guided light wave transmission.

Eligibility: 10+2 /12th with Maths

Courses:

B. Tech   M. Tech

Institutes & Universities:

IIT

Salary:

The annual salary in India is around INR 3.5Lakhs to INR 4.5Lakhs. With some experience, you can earn between INR 5 – 9Lakhs a year. In abroad, the mean annual salaries for ceramic engineers will be $60k to $80K.

For more information you may visit the website below:
https://www.ceramtec.com/

*"**Mr. Mokshagundam Visvesvaraya:** A Famous Personality who really made it Big in the world of Ceramics Engineering"*

CIVIL ENGINEERING

It deals with planning, drawing and executing construction of buildings like bridges, homes, bridges, etc. This offers challenging career opportunities who are talented and focused to create innovative structures. The major specialization areas in this field are structural, drainage environmental, transportation, geotechnical engineering etc.

Future Prospects: Even though the number of graduates are more in this field and less paid but chances of getting a high salary is more. It is due to high demand and paid for innovation and talent in this field.

Eligibility: 10+2 /12th with Maths
Courses:

B. Tech	M. Tech
Ph.D

Institutes & Universities:

AMU, Aligadh	BHU, Varanasi
Government Engineering College, Aurangabad	IIT-Mumbai, Delhi, Kharagpur

Salary:
The average annual salary for a Civil Engineer is around 4-6Lakhs in India.
For more information you may visit the website below:
https://www.getmyuni.com/civil-engineering-colleges

COMPUTER SCIENCE ENGINEERING

During 1980's, it was highly in demand and those who graduated went to the USA, abroad and settled there. Still there is growing demand for this field which involves software and hardware. You may be a super specialized in this area. This sector is growing due to the rise of new demands in areas like cybercrime, demand for programming, BPO etc.

Future Prospects: Now there is huge competition in India and International market. If you want to come in this industry, you need to be committed and ready to do hard work in an innovative manner.

Eligibility: 10+2 /12th with Maths & Chemistry

Courses:

B. Tech Computer Science & Engineering   M. Tech

Ph.D

Institutes & Universities:

IIT – Mumbai, Delhi, Kanpur, Kharagpur

Smt. Savitribai Phule University of Pune

University of Mumbai

Salary:

After obtaining a degree in CSE, you can expect handsome salary packages in government as well as private sector. The IT sector is the higher salary providing sector. A fresher can get the initial package of 4-7Lakh per annum in India.

For more information you may visit the website below:
https://www.shiksha.com/engineering/computer-science-engineering-chp

*"**Mr. Alan Turing:** A Famous Personality who really made it Big in the world of Computer Science Engineering"*

ELECTRICAL & ELECTRONICS ENGINEERING

It deals with power generation, power distribution, creation of new electrical and electronic equipment for the benefit of humanity. Now new technology is coming forward for the generation of electricity like solar, etc.

Future Prospects: Now electricity is moving from non- renewable to renewable energy like solar, wind energy, etc. Hence engineers have to focus on it and learn those things to remain dynamic in the changing world. Also, the value of engineers is increasing in this sector.

Eligibility: 10+2 /12th with Maths
Courses:

B. Tech   M. Tech

Ph.D

Institutes & Universities:

BHU, Varanasi   IIT – Mumbai, Delhi, Kanpur, Kharagpur

Salary:
The average salary for an Electrical Engineer is 3-5 lakh per annum in India.
For more information you may visit the website below:
https://www.careers360.com/courses/electrical-and-electronics-engineering-course

*"**Mr. Stephen Gary Wozniak:** A Famous Personality who really made it Big in the world of Electrical & Electronics Engineering"*

ELECTRONICS & COMMUNICATION ENGINEERING

It deals with development of communication technology in perspective of television, radio, media, radio, computers and band spectrum with the use of electronic technology. This helps to increase productivity through efficiency and reduces time for completion of technology.

Future Prospects: It has great prospects due to the rise of demand for media, mobile & communication technology. Hence demand for fresh graduates ultimately would increase.

Eligibility: 10+2 /12th with Maths

Courses:

B.E. in Electronics & Communication

M.E. in Electronics & Communication

Ph.D

Institutes & Universities:

Bharati Vidhyapeeth's College of Engineering

BML Munjal University, Gurgaon

Delhi Technological University

Dr. B.R. Ambedkar Institute of Advanced Communication Technologies & Research

IIT - Mumbai, Delhi, Kanpur, Kharagpur

Indraprastha Institute of Information Technology

Jamia Millia Islamia University

Salary:

The average annual salary of freshers includes INR. 4 to 4.5Lakhs per year. Electronics students with skills in robotics, automation technologies, renewable energies, Internet of Things (IoT), mechatronics engineering concepts add more value to their average pay scale.

*"**Mr. James Clerk Maxwell:** A Famous Personality who really made it Big in the world of Electronics & Communications Engineering"*

INFORMATION, COMMUNICATION & ENTERTAINMENT (ICE)

This is the age of Information, Communication and Entertainment (ICE). The massive expansion in broadcasting with the introduction of more television channels, direct broadcast satellites, T.V./Computer link ups, cable T.V. and rapid growth in both All India Radio and other broadcasting services particularly FM boosts this sector.

Eligibility: 10+2 /12th with Science, Commerce or Arts

Courses:

- B.A. in Mass Communication
- B.A. in Journalism

Institutes & Universities:

- Chitabani, Kolkata
- Indian Institute of Mass Communication, JNU Campus-New Delhi
- Indraprastha College for Mass Communication, New Delhi
- International Institute of Information Technology - Hyderabad
- Mass Communication Research Centre, Jamia Millia Islamia University
- Xaviers Institute of Communication

Salary:
The average salary for a Reporter is 3-4 lakh per annum in India. For more information you may visit the website below:
https://kpmg.com/pk/en/home/industries/telecommunications.html

INSTRUMENTATION ENGINEERING

It deals with computing instruments which deals designing and using for dynamic processing.

Eligibility: 10+2 /12th with Maths

Courses:

- B.E. & B. Tech
- M.E. & M. Tech
- M. Phil
- Ph.D

Institutes & Universities:

Bangalore Institute of Technology, Karnataka

IIT - Mumbai, Delhi

Bharati Vidyapeeth College of Engineering, Maharashtra

M. S. Ramaiah Institute of Technology, Karnataka

Salary:

The average salary is around 6-8Lakh per annum in India.
For more information you may visit the website below:
https://engineering.careers360.com/articles/instrumentation-technology-0

The human race has seen unbelievable progress and development as we've moved from the era of cavemen to the current age of smartphones. It would only be fair to say that if any one community has played a significant part in making this happen, it is the engineering community. Had it not been for the toil and brains of all the successful engineers of the past as well as present, we couldn't have developed and found ourselves in the advanced age we currently enjoy.

Listed below are some of the great Indian Engineers and their notable contributions in shaping society as we know it today. Engineers apply theories of science to solve practical problems in the world around them. India is known for producing notable engineers since the times of M. Visvesvaraya in the 1860s. He is considered as one of the greatest Indian Engineers and was bestowed with Bharat Ratna in 1955. His contribution was beyond the realms of engineering infrastructures as he was a significant influencer in setting up several industries. The various sectors including iron & steel, soaps, silk, sugar, banking & aeronautics.

Let us look at some of them, and the mark they made on society:

Sundar Pichai

The current CEO of Google Technology Inc, Sundar Pichai is a computer engineer. He was bright and creative from a young age and worked in Engineering and Product Management at Applied Materials and in Management Consulting at McKinsey & Company before he joined Google. Pichai is known for being the mastermind behind the launch of the Chrome browser in 2008.

Narayan Murthy

One of the brilliant minds behind the Indian multinational company Infosys Ltd, Narayan Murthy is counted amongst the greatest industrialists of contemporary times. Under his leadership, Infosys became the first Indian company to feature on Nasdaq.

E Shreedharan

Elattuvalapil Sreedharan, popularly known as the "Metro Man", is an Indian engineer who played a key role in changing the face of public transport in India, particularly his work behind building the Konkan Railway and the Delhi Metro. For his path breaking work in the development of Delhi Metro he was awarded with the Padma Vibhushan, the second highest civilian award in the Republic of India, in 2018.

MECHANICAL ENGINEERING

It deals with application of mechanics for developments of automobiles, trucks, machinery, formulation of mechanical structure of vehicle etc. Also, it has specialisations like Cryogenic technology, Laser material processing, Robotics, Advanced vehicle designing etc.

Eligibility: 10+2 /12th with Maths

Courses:

B.E. Mechanical *M. Tech*

Ph.D

Institutes & Universities:

College of Engineering, Pune *Delhi University*

Government College of Engineering, Aurangabad *IIT - Mumbai, Delhi, Kanpur*

Jawaharlal Nehru University (JNU), Delhi *Smt. Savitribai Phule University of Pune*

Salary:

The average salary is around 4-6 lakh per annum in India.

For more information you may visit the website below:

https://www.shiksha.com/engineering/mechanical-engineering-chp

*"**Mr. Sushanta Kumar Bhattacharya**: A Famous Personality who really made it Big in the world of Mechanical Engineering"*

METEOROLOGY

It deals in predicting weather and climate. It is sub-disciple of atmospheric sciences. A sub-discipline is a specialized field of study within a broader subject or discipline. This is going to become an important field in the future.

Eligibility: 10+2 /12th with PCM

Courses:

B.Tech/B.Sc   M. Tech/ M.Sc

Ph.D

Institutes & Universities:

BHU, Varanasi   College of Engineering, Pune

IIT - Mumbai, Delhi, Roorkee, Kharagpur, West Bengal   Shivaji University, Maharashtra

Salary:
The average salary is around 4-6Lakhs per annum in India.
For more information you may visit the website below:
https://www.nationalgeographic.org/encyclopedia/meteorology/

MINING ENGINEERING

It deals with the technology to extract and process minerals from the Earth's surroundings. It includes study of all operations and planning, drilling, ventilation and other activities.

Eligibility: 10+2 /12th with PCM
Courses:

B.E. in Mining *B.Tech in Mining*
M.E. in Mining *M.Tech in Mining*
Ph.D in Mining

Institutes & Universities:

Government Engineering College, Bilaspur-Chhattisgarh

IIT - Mumbai, Delhi, kanpur, Kharagpur

Jay Narain Vyas University, Jodhpur-Rajasthan

Maharana Pratap University of Agriculture & Technology, Jodhpur-Rajasthan

Rashtrasant Tukadoji Maharaj University of Nagpur, Nagpur-Maharashtra

Salary:
The average salary is around 6-8Lakhs per annum in India.
For more information you may visit the website below:
https://collegedunia.com/courses/bachelor-of-engineering-be-mining-engineering

NAVAL ARCHITECTURE ENGINEERING

It is concerned with planning, preparing design, construction of boats, ships, submarines and maintenance of all above. This is the most demanding sector in the defense especially for the Government of India. These all focus on the technical side of the Navy.

Eligibility: 10+2 /12th with PCM
Courses:

B.E. *B.Tech*
M.Tech

Institutes & Universities:

IIT - Chennai, Kharagpur *Institute of Shipbuilding, Goa*

Kochi University of Science & Technology

Salary:
The average salary is around 6-10Lakhs per annum in India.
For more information you may visit the website below:
https://www.marineinsight.com/naval-architecture/what-is-naval-architecture/

POLYMER ENGINEERING

It deals with the formulation of material and application to a wide range of things like packing of materials, construction of buildings, clothes, plastics which are utilized for the vehicles. This has a great future where you can show your talent through your innovative ideas.

Eligibility: 10+2 /12th with PCM

Institutes & Universities:
IIT - Mumbai, Delhi *Birla*

Courses:

B.E. *B.Tech*
M.E. *M.Tech*
Ph.D

Salary:
In the case of the private sector, a polymer engineering professional can expect a monthly salary ranging from INR. 3-4Lakh per annum at an entry-level.
For more information you may visit the website below:
https://www.indiaeducation.net/careercenter/engineering/polymerengineering/

ROBOTICS

It is a field where many things are collaborated like Computer Engineering, Mechanical Engg., Electrical Engineering, Machine learning, etc. It's used along with artificial intelligence for the benefit of humanity. And where humanity cannot reach it is also utilized for space, medical surgeries, mining. Also vastly used where humans have a risk to their life.

Now the world is moving towards automation where all things run automatically with the help of artificial intelligence, machine learning, etc. There is a great future for those who want to make a career in this field.

Eligibility: 10+2 /12th with PCM
Courses:
   B.Tech   M.Tech
   Ph.D

Institutes & Universities:
   Birla Institute of Technology & Science, Pilani-Mesra
   IISC, Bangalore
   IIT - Mumbai, Delhi, kanpur, Kharagpur, Chennai

Salary:
In India, as a Robotics Engineer you can easily earn a starting salary between INR. 13 to 14Lakh per year. More experience will help you to earn more in this field.

For more information you may visit the website below:
https://www.shiksha.com/engineering/robotics-engineering-chp

Names of Top Robotics Scientists & Engineers.in World

   Brian Gerkey, CEO of the Open-Source Robotics Foundation

   Colin Angle, CEO of iRobot

   Cynthia Breazeal, director of MIT Media Lab's Personal Robots Group

   Daniela Rus, director of MIT's Computer Science and Artificial Intelligence Lab

Hiroshi Ishiguro, director of the Intelligent Robotics Laboratory, at Osaka University, Japan

Melonee Wise, CEO of Unbounded Robotics

Raj Reddy, professor of computer science at Carnegie Mellon University

Steve Cousins, CEO of Savioke and formerly of Willow Garage

Marc Raibert, founder of Google-owned Boston Dynamics

Niranjan C.G, CEO of Nizan Robotics Pvt Ltd. Coimbatore

Ryan Calo, Assistant Professor of Law at University of Washington

TEXTILE ENGINEERING

It focusses on formulation and creation of fibers, textile products, clothing formulation, its machinery, etc. This sector is mainly related with the production of clothes.

Eligibility: 10+2 /12th with PCM

Courses:
B.Tech *M.Tech*
Post Graduate Diploma

Institutes & Universities:
Mumbai University, Department of Chemical Technology

IIT-Delhi

Institute of Textile Technology, Cuttack-Orissa

Salary:
The salary increases with experience and skills. Experienced candidates can earn even more than Rs. 12 -14 lakh per annum apart from other incentives and perks.
For more information you may visit the website below:
https://collegedunia.com/courses/bachelor-of-technology-btech-textile-engineering

*"**Mr. Rajha, the Chairman of Ramco Group:** A Famous Personality who really made it Big in the world of Textile Engineering"*

AGRICULTURAL SCIENCE

It mainly focuses on study of agriculture, high production of agriculture products, and how to increase the productivity of land and plants. Now it is a growing field in the area of agricultural banking and scientific growth.

Eligibility: 10+2 /12th with PCB

Courses:

B.Sc in Agriculture

B.Sc in Fisheries Science (B.F.Sc)

B.Sc in Food Technology

Bachelor in Biotechnology

M.Sc in Agriculture

Ph.D

Institutes & Universities:

CCS Agriculture University, Hisar-Haryana

University of Agricultural Sciences, Bangalore

Marathwada Agricultural University, Parbhani-Maharashtra

University of Agriculture, Akola-Maharashtra

Salary:
Currently the salary of an entry level ICAR Scientist (Agricultural Research Service) is equivalent to Assistant Professor scale of UGC i.e. 15600–39100 Grade Pay 6000 Rs (as per the Sixth pay commission)

For more information you may visit the website below:
https://www.indiaeducation.net/agriculture/

*"**Dr. M. S. Swaminathan:** A Famous Personality who really made it Big in the world of Agricultural Science"*

BIO-TECHNOLOGY

This sector is the utilized combination of Engineering, Biology, Chemistry, Machine Learning to produce and development of new living cells, drugs, organs through Biotechnology. This has many super-specializations like, Tissue Culture, Human Genetics with Plant Genetics Engineering, Drug Development, Human Organ Development, etc.

Eligibility: 10+2 /12th with PCB

Courses:

B. Sc   *M. Sc*

Ph.D

Salary:
The Government of India provides large-scale employment to most biotechnologists in its research laboratories. Those employed as researchers in the government sector can have a starting salary of Rs 75000/- month starting gross.
For more information you may visit the website below:
https://www.sarvgyan.com/courses/engineering/biotechnology-engineering

COMPUTER APPLICATION

This is a very interesting area of Computer Technology where you have scope to apply your knowledge for the development of various applications. Under these various applications are developed for the benefit of humanity which make life simple and fast.

Eligibility: 10+2 /12th with PCM

Courses:
- Bachelor in Computer Application
- Master in Computer Application
- Ph.D

Institutes & Universities:
- IIT- Mumbai, Delhi, Kanpur
- University of Madras, Chennai
- University of Allahabad
- University of Mumbai

Note: *Computer Application Courses are also offered by various private institutions. Therefore, aspirants are advised to ensure the recognition and approved courses prior to admission.*

Salary:
The MCA course salary on average ranges from 4.5 to 6.5 lakhs per annum to an MCA course student depending upon work organization and education skills. Both the private and government sectors hire qualified MCA course graduates for a job.
For more information you may visit the website below:
https://www.inc.com/encyclopedia/computer-applications.html

COMPUTER SCIENCE

This has two important specializations like hardware and software. Hardware focuses on the manufacturing of computers, whereas software is related with development of Computer Applications. This is a continuous growing field where a person has a lot of scope if you are talented and ready to do hard work.

Eligibility: 10+2 /12th with PCM

Courses:

B.Tech	M.Tech
B.SC(CS, IT, IS)	BCA
MCA	Ph.D

Institutes & Universities:

IIT-Mumbai, Bangalore, Kharagpur, Kanpur

Salary:

The average salary for a Computer Scientist is more than 5 lakhs a month or more, SKY's the limit in India.
For more information you may visit the website below:
https://www.khanacademy.org/computing/computer-science

CYBER SECURITY

It is a growing field in the present scenario due to increasing threats in financial persona, technical, industrial and in all sensitive matters. It includes, introduction of computer viruses into the system, phishing, illegal hacking of systems, illegal transfer of money from the bank accounts, defence breach etc.

Eligibility: 10+2 /12th with PCM

Courses:

B.Tech	M.Tech
Ph.D	

Institutes & Universities:

IIT-Mumbai, Hyderabad, Delhi, Guwahati, Allahabad, Kanpur

Salary:

The salary of a cyber security analyst begins at Rs 10 to 15 lakhs per annum.

Note: *Yes, it's a small wonder why cyber security experts are in high demand. In fact, ISACA, a non-profit information security advocacy group, predicted that there will be a global shortage of two million cyber security professionals by 2019.*

For more information you may visit the website below:
https://mind-core.com/5-types-of-cyber-security/

EARTH SCIENCE/ GEOGRAPHY

It deals with the earth's structure, examination of the earth's atmosphere and its protection. Also, it concerns natural resources like air, water, clouds, weather forecasting, etc.

Eligibility: 10+2 /12th from any stream

Courses:
- B.A
- M. A
- Ph.D

Institutes & Universities:

- IIT-Roorkee
- Indian Institute of Science, Bangalore

Salary:
The salary of the students ranges from Rs. 5 lakhs to Rs. 10 lakh per month depending upon the sector one has joined.
For more information you may visit the website below:
https://www.hotcoursesabroad.com/india/training-degrees/international/earth-sciences-geography-teaching-courses/cgory/gc.89-4/sin/ct/programs.html

*"**Dame Evelyn Mary Stokes:** A Famous Personality who really made it Big in the world of Geography"*

ENVIRONMENTAL SCIENCE

This sector is becoming a hot subject in today's scenario due to concern of climate change. This concern rises due to change in climate and biological structure of the environment.

Eligibility: 10+2 /12th with PCB

Courses:

B. Sc   *M. Sc*
Ph.D

Institutes & Universities:

Babasaheb Bhimrao Ambedkar University, Lucknow-UP

Delhi University

School of Environmental Science, JNU

University of Mumbai

Salary:
The average salary for an Environmental Scientist range in between 5 to 7 lakhs per annum.
For more information you may visit the website below:
https://www.topuniversities.com/courses/environmental-studies/guide

FOOD TECHNOLOGY

It deals with production of safe nutritious food products. These also focus on high food productivity with rich ingredients at lower cost and short span of time.

Eligibility: 10+2 /12th with PCB or PCM
Courses:

B.Tech   *M.Tech*
Ph.D

Institutes & Universities:

Delhi University

Dr. Babasaheb Ambedkar Marathwada University, Aurangabad

*Marathwada Agricultural
University, Parbhani-
Maharashtra*

Salary:
Salary Structure of a Food Technologist in Food Industry in India: As a fresher, a Food Technologist can earn INR Rs 6 to 8 lakh per annum (average) in India. Within 5 years, you can reach INR 800,000 – 150,0000 per annum.
For more information you may visit the website below:
https://www.sarvgyan.com/courses/engineering/food-technology

FORESTRY

It mainly focuses on the development of forest in the benefit of humanity like protection of forest, development of plants, growth of forest land, protection of tribal population, etc. This helps to protect endangered species and provide clean air with water

Eligibility: 10+2 /12th with PCB or PCM

Courses:

B.Sc in Forestry / Wildlife

M.Sc in Forestry / Wildlife / Forest Economics

Institutes & Universities:

Agricultural College & Research Institute, Coimbatore

Gujarat Agricultural University

Marathwada Agricultural University, Parbhani-Maharashtra

Orissa University of Agriculture & Technology

Punjab Agricultural University

Salary:
The average salary for a Forest Officer in the Government of India ranges from 10 to 13 lakhs per annum.
For more information you may visit the website below:
https://study.com/academy/lesson/what-is-forestry-definition-types.html

Popular Forest Ranges in India

Arunachal Pradesh Forest

Jim Corbett National Park, Uttarakhand

Khasi Hills, Meghalaya

Sundarban Forests, West Bengal

Gir Forest, Gujarat

Kaziranga Forest, Assam

Nilgiri Biosphere Reserve, Tamil Nadu

Vandalur Forest Reserve

OCEANOGRAPHY

It deals with the physical and biological structure of the ocean with focus on plants and animals under the sea.

Eligibility: 10+2 /12th with PCB or PCM

Courses:

M.Sc in Oceanography & Coastal Area Studies

M.Tech in Ocean Technology

Institutes & Universities:

Mangalore University, Bangalore

University Of Goa

University of Science & Technology, Cochin-Kerala

Salary:

In India, the salary of an oceanographer starts from Rs 4-5 Lakhs per annum.

For more information you may visit the website below:

https://www.environmentalscience.org/career/oceanographer

MATHEMATICS & STATISTICAL SCIENCE

Statistics is the study data and navigating common problems for drawing correct conclusions. This course is related to the field such as areas in financial markets, sports, engineering, healthcare, marketing & sales, election campaigns, space, natural disasters, population studies, accidents, insurance, and deaths – statistics. Statistics deals with interpretation and aggregation of large complex data into simpler data. It is developed from the field of probability in mathematics.

Eligibility: 10+2 /12th with PCM

Courses:

- Bachelor of Mathematics (Honours)
- Bachelor of Statistics (Honours)
- Diploma in Maths with Computer Programming
- Bachelor in Statistical Methods
- Diploma in Applied Mathematics

Institutes & Universities:

- Chennai Mathematical Institute, Chennai
- IIT- Kharagpur
- Tata Institute of Fundamental Research, Mumbai
- College of Engineering, Chennai
- Osmania University, Hyderabad

Salary:

The average salary for a statistician, range from 7 to 9 lakhs per annum.

For more information you may visit the website below:
https://www.ualberta.ca/mathematical-and-statistical-sciences/index.html

Mathematics is the art of giving the same name to different things...

WILDLIFE BIOLOGY

This is related to protection of animals in their natural area with observation of the wildlife animals. This also includes working in the laboratory and in a different environment.

Eligibility: 10+2 /12th with PCB

Courses:

- Bachelor in Wildlife Biology
- Masters in Wildlife Biology

Institutes & Universities:

- Institute of Environment Education & Research, Bharati Vidyapeet, Pune-Maharashtra
- National Centre for Biological Science, Bangalore-Karnataka

Salary:
In India, the salary ranges from Rs 5-6 Lakhs per annum.
For more information you may visit the website below:
https://www.deepjunglehome.in/list-of-colleges-and-universities-offering-wildlife-biology/

India has been home to some incredible wildlife warriors like Valmik Thapar, Romulus Whitaker, Uma Ramakrishnan, Prerna Singh Bindra, Latika Nath, Bittu Sahgal and K. Ullas Karanth, to name a few, who have spent their lives working, writing and fighting for conservation and raising awareness about India's Wildlife animals.

MBBS

This is the most demanding medical area where all parents and students like to pursue their career after 12th Class. After completing MBBS there is a huge competition for admission in super-speciality fields like Gynaecology, Paediatrics, Surgery, Medicine, Ophthalmology, etc.

Eligibility: 10+2 /12th with PCB

Courses:

MBBS	MD
MS	MS (Ortho.)

Institutes & Universities:

AIIMS, Delhi	Government Medical College, Nagpur
J.J Medical College, Mumbai	K.E.M Medical College, Mumbai

Salary:
It can range from Rs 9-12 lakh per annum for a doctor who has just finished his MBBS.
For more information you may visit the website below:
https://medicine.careers360.com/colleges/ranking
https://collegedunia.com/mbbs-colleges

AYURVEDA - BAMS

Ayurveda is a system of medicine developed in India before 1000 BC from where other doctors used to learn from other countries. Like surgeon Sushruta during that period had done surgeries like Eye, etc. Today, the value and curiosity about the Ayurveda is increasing due to fast inclination towards natural life and Yoga.

Eligibility: 10+2 /12th with PCB

Courses:

Bachelor of Ayurvedic Medicine & Surgery (BAMS)

Masters in Ayurveda (MD)

Ph. D

Institutes & Universities:

All India Institute of Ayurveda, New Delhi

Ayurvedic & Unani Tibbia College & Hospital, New Delhi

Government Ayurvedic College, Ahmedabad-Gujarat

Government Ayurvedic College, Nagpur-Maharashtra

Government Ayurvedic College & Hospital, Lucknow-UP

National Institute of Ayurveda, Jaipur-Rajasthan

R.A. Podar Medical College, Mumbai

Salary:
The remuneration of an Ayurvedic doctor appointed in a government hospital/department is similar to that of a homeopathic doctor. The gross salary varies between Rs. 7-8 lakh/annum.

For more information you may visit the website below:
https://collegedunia.com/courses/bachelor-of-ayurvedic-medicine-and-surgery-bams

DENTAL - BDS

It is related to teeth treatment along with gums, hard and soft tissues of mouth, cosmetic surgery, plastic surgery, etc. There are super-speciality areas like Orthodontics (straightening and aligning teeth and jaws), oral pathology, etc.

Eligibility: 10+2 /12th with PCB

Courses:

Bachelor of Dental Surgery (BDS)

Masters in Dental Surgery (MS)

Institutes & Universities:

Faculty of Dentistry, Jamia Millia Islamia University, New Delhi

Government Dental College, Mumbai

Government Dental College, Mumbai

Maulana Azad Dental College & Hospital, New Delhi

Salary:
In India, the salary ranges from Rs 5-6 Lakhs per annum.
For more information you may visit the website below:
http://ymtdental.org/MDS_FEE1.html

HOMEOPATHY - BHMS

It is German medical system which is practised in most countries in the world. It focuses on healing the patient by restoring all elements of body parts. The medicines are prepared with diluted parts of natural resources which are like the elements in the human body. It includes all other subjects which are available in MBBS except Pharmacology (Medicine).

Eligibility: 10+2 /12th with PCB

Courses:

Bachelor of Homeopathic Medicine & Surgery (BHMS)

Masters in Homeopathic Medicine & Surgery (MD)

Institutes & Universities:

Homeopathic Medical College, Hyderabad

Salary:
In the government sector the starting salary of a homeopathic doctor is around 5 to 6 lakhs per annum.
For more information you may visit the website below:
https://collegedunia.com/medical/homeopathy-colleges

NATUROPATHY

This uses nature to heal humans with natural elements. It focuses on five elements which considers the body is made up of these elements like air, water, earth, aether and fire. It considers whenever there is disturbance in its balance, there would be disease in the body. Naturopathy then focuses on balancing its elements to cure disease. Also, Yoga is an important part in this to heal the body which they consider to balance these elements.

Eligibility: 10+2 /12th with PCB

Courses:

B.SC

Bachelor of Naturopathy & Yogic Science (BNYS)

MD

Institutes & Universities:

Banaras Hindu University, Varanasi

Morarji Desai National Institute of Yoga, New Delhi

National Institute of Naturopathy, Pune

Salary:

Starting salary of a Naturopathy doctor is around 3 to 4 lakhs per annum.

For more information you may visit the website below:
https://collegedunia.com/courses/bachelor-of-naturopathy-and-yoga-science-colleges

*"**Dr. B. D. Patel:** A Famous Personality who really made it Big in the world of Naturopathy"*

PHARMACY

It deals with the study of drugs, formulation of new drugs, studying composition, effects, side effects of drugs on the human body, etc. It also focuses on development and standardization of new drugs.

Eligibility: 10+2 /12th with PCB

Courses:
B.Pharma   M. Pharma
Ph.D

Institutes & Universities:

AMU, Aligarh

BHU, Varanasi

Jamia Hamdard, New Delhi

Mumbai University

National Institute of Pharmaceutical Education & Research, Mohali

Smt. Savitribai Phule University of Pune, Pune

Salary:
Starting salary of a pharmacist is around 3 to 4 lakhs per annum.
For more information you may visit the website below:
https://collegedunia.com/pharmacy-colleges

*"**Dr. Mahadev Lal:** A Famous Personality who really made it Big in the world of Pharmacy"*

SIDDHA

This medicine system is developed in south India which is a very old system and it is growing in popularity. It also worked like Naturopathy where they focus on five elements like water, earth, fire and sky for treatment of disease. It is a growing field under AYUSH, DEPARTMENT UNDER GOVERNMENT OF INDIA.

Eligibility: 10+2 /12th with PCB

Courses:

- Bachelor of Siddha Medicine & Science (BSMS)
- MD

Institutes & Universities:

- AkilaThiruvithamcore Siddha VaidhyaSamgam, Siddha MaruthuvaKalloory& Hospital, Kanyakumari
- Government Siddha Medical College, Tirunelveli
- National Institute of Siddha, Chennai
- Santhigiri Siddha Medical College, Thiruvananthapuram
- Velumailu Siddha Medical College & Hospital, Kanchipuram
- Government Siddha Medical College, Chennai
- Kerala University of Health Sciences, Thrissur-Kerala
- RVS Siddha Medical College, Coimbatore
- Sri Sai Ram Siddha Medical College & Research, Chennai

Salary:

Starting salary is around 3 lakhs per annum.

For more information you may visit the website below:

https://www.gyanunlimited.com/education/siddha-colleges-institutions-and-institutes-in-india/1739/

UNANI

It is popular in Greece, Arabian countries, etc. This originated in Greece around 500 BC. It works on 'HUMORAL THERAPY' in which it works on four bodily fluids which compose body parts. For treatment, medicine is prepared from minerals, plants, animal parts, earth elements etc.

Eligibility: 10+2 /12th with PCB

Courses:

Bachelor of Unani Medicine & Surgery (BUMS)
MD

Institutes & Universities:

Aligarh Muslim University, Aligarh
BHU, Varanasi
Delhi University
Mumbai University
National Institute of Unani Medicine, Bangalore

Salary:

In the government sector the starting salary of a Unani doctor is around 5-6 lakh per annum.

For more information you may visit the website below:
https://collegedunia.com/bums-colleges

ANTHROPOLOGY

This deals with the biological and physical structure of humans with respect to culture, environment in past, present and future. It also study, evolution of humans from earlier to present.

Eligibility: 10+2 /12th with PCB or PCM

Courses:

B.A / B.Sc
M.A / M.Sc
Ph.D

Institutes & Universities:

BHU, Varanasi
Delhi University
Sambalpur University, Orissa
Smt. Savitribai Phule University of Pune, Pune

Salary:

One can expect a salary in the range around 2-3 lakh per annum.
For more information you may visit the website below:
https://collegedunia.com/ba/anthropology-colleges

ARCHAELOGY & ART RESTORATION

In this, students reconstruct extinct cultures from old structures on the basis of historical facts. In art restoration, it focuses on protection and restoration of old art structure with the help of modern technology.

Eligibility: 10+2 /12th with Arts & History

Courses:

- B.A
- M.A
- Ph. D

Institutes & Universities:

- Delhi Institute of Heritage Research Management, New Delhi
- Institute of Archaeology, New Delhi
- National Museum Institute, New Delhi

Salary:

An Art Conservator initially can expect Rs 2-2.5 lakh per annum. For more information you may visit the website below:

https://www.jagranjosh.com/articles/top-courses-in-art-restoration-152654

EDUCATION COUNSELLOR

It is very important for students to manage their problems in behavioural, academic or school activities. This is helped through counselling activities done to students as well as to parents by a counsellor.

Eligibility: Graduate or Master's Degree

Courses:

- Certificate Course in Counselling & Guidance
- B.A / M.A in Psychology, Child Development or Social Work

Institutes & Universities:

- Indira Gandhi National Open University, New Delhi
- Mumbai University
- National Council of Edu. Research & Training, New Delhi
- National Institute of Public Cooperation & Child Development, New Delhi

For more information you may visit the website below:
https://www.campusexplorer.com/careers/225B1239/educational-vocational-and-school-counselors/

MONUMENTS & SCULPTURE RESTORATION

In this, monuments and sculptures are restored through a professional way. Also, damaged structure is repaired and maintained.

Eligibility: 10+2 /12th with Arts & History

Courses:

B.A   *M.A*

Ph.D

Institutes & Universities:

Delhi Institute of Heritage Research & Management, New Delhi

Sinhgad College of Architecture, Pune

Salary:

Fine Art restorers are paid around 10 lakhs per annum.

For more information you may visit the website below:
https://www.jagranjosh.com/articles/top-courses-in-art-restoration-1526543506-1

STATUE OF UNITY

The Statue of Unity is a colossal statue of Indian statesman and independence activist Shri Sardar Vallabhai Patel (15–1950), who was the first Home-Minister of independent India and the chief adherent of Mahatma Gandhi during the non-violent Indian Independence Movement.

He was highly respected for his leadership in uniting the 552 princely states of India to form a single Union of India. It is located in the state of Gujarat, India. It is the world's tallest statue with a height of 182 metres. It is located on a river island facing the Sardar Sarovar Dam on river Narmada in Kevadiya Colony, 100 kilometres (62 mi) southeast of the city of

Vadodara and 150 km from Surat.

The project was first announced in 2010 and the construction of the statue started in October 2013 by L&T, who received the contract for ₹2,989 crore (US$420 million) from the Government of Gujarat. It was designed by Indian sculptor Ram V. Sutar, and was inaugurated by Prime Minister of India, Mr. Narendra Modi on 31 October 2018, the 143rd birth anniversary of Sardar Patel.

*"**Mr. Ram V Sutar:** A Famous Personality who really made it Big in the world of Sculpture"*

MUSEOLOGY

It deals with development and organisation of museums with its knowledge. It also focuses on activities such as preservation, restoration and excavation of ancient monuments and the art material.

Eligibility: 10+2 /12th with Arts & History

Courses:
B.A
M.A
Ph.D

Institutes & Universities:
Aligarh Muslim University, Aligarh-UP

Bharatiya Kala Nidhi, Institute of Archaeology, ASI, New Delhi

National Museum Institute of History of Art, Conservation & Museology, New Delhi

For more information you may visit the website below:
http://nmi.gov.in/departmentsmuseologycourses.htm

*"**Ayinapalli Aiyappan**: A Famous Personality who really made it Big in world of the Museology"*

PHYSIOTHERAPY

This therapy deals with restoration of physical disability, restoring original health through physical therapies. It is a growing field and demanding due to high results in patient's health. It uses the techniques of examination, evaluation and diagnosis.

Eligibility: 10+2 /12th with PCB

Courses:

Bachelor of Physiotherapy (BPT)   Master of Physiotherapy (MPT)

Institutes & Universities:

Government Medical College, Nagpur-Maharashtra

Indian Institute of Health Education & Research, Patna-Bihar

Nizam's Institute of Medical Sciences, Hyderabad

Salary:
An average salary starts from Rs 2-3 lakh per annum.
For more information you may visit the website below:
https://collegedunia.com/bachelor-of-physiotherapy-colleges

SOCIAL WORK

This studies social problems like unemployment, injustice, poverty, human trafficking and solve problems with help of government and society.

Eligibility: 10+2 /12th for any stream

Courses:

B.A   BSW

MSW

Institutes & Universities:

Bangalore University	Delhi School of Social Work, Delhi
Milind College, Aurangabad-Maharashtra	Mumbai University
Osmania University, Hyderabad	

Salary:
An average salary starts from Rs 2-3 lakh per annum.
For more information you may visit the website below:
https://collegedunia.com/arts/social-work-colleges

LAW

It is a study of rules, regulations, constitution of nation, criminal law, civil law, etc. Law has many super specialised areas where lawyers can do specialization for his career. It is always a demanding career after 10+2 with any subject for an integrated course of five years.

Eligibility: 10+2 /12th any stream

Courses:

LLB   LLM

LLD

Institutes & Universities:

Government Law College, Mumbai	Indian Law School, Pune
Mumbai University	National Academy of Legal Studies & Research University of Law (NALSAR), Hyderabad
National Law School of India University (NLSIU), Bangalore	National Law University (NLU), Jodhpur-Rajasthan

Smt. Savitribai Phule University of Pune, Pune

Salary:

In India, the range of salary that the law firms offer ranges all the way from Rs 10-30 lakh per annum. Even for lawyers who have just graduated from college, there is a wide potential range from between Rs 3-5 lakh per year.

For more information you may visit the website below:

https://www.shiksha.com/law/ranking/top-law-colleges-in-india/56-2-0-0-0

*"**Dr. B.R. Ambedkar.** A Famous Personality who really made it Big in the world of Law"*

ADVERTISING

It deals with raising demand for products through rise in marketing, linking customers with products. This helps in influencing customers to attract towards the product and make them purchase it. This can be done through various mediums like new paper, televisions, journals, magazines, etc.

This is a growing field with high perks and salary. With proper education and experience, you can have a great future.

Eligibility: 10+2 /12th any stream

Courses:

Diploma in Advertising

MBA in Advertising, Public Relations, Sales & Marketing

Integrated BA. In Advertising, Sales, Promotion & Management

Post-Graduation Diploma in Advertising

Institutes & Universities:

Annamalai University, Chennai

IGNOU, Delhi

Xavier Institute of Communications, Mumbai

Delhi University

Indian Institute of Mass Communication, JNU-New Delhi

Salary:
In India, the range of salary for an Advertising Manager is around Rs 3-4 lakhs per annum.
For more information you may visit the website below:
https://www.jagranjosh.com/institutes-colleges/journalism-mass-commun

MEDIA, MASS COMMUNICATION & JOURNALISM

It focuses on preparation of written, visual, or audio material for dissemination through public media like writing, audio, audio-visual etc. They do it through TV, radio, print media etc. This has a great future due to increasing demand & increasing private companies in these areas.

Eligibility: 10+2 /12th any stream

Courses:

Bachelor of Journalism (B.J)

Bachelor of Mass Media (B.M.M)

Bachelor of Journalism & Mass Communication (B.J.M.C)

Masters of Journalism (M.J)

Salary:
Starting salary for a mass communication professional could be around Rs 3-4 lakhs per annum.
For more information you may visit the website below:
https://www.shiksha.com/mass-communication-media/ranking/top-mass-communication-colleges-in-india/99-2-0-0-0

Some of the Best Journalists in India:

Arnab Goswami
Josy Joseph
Minhaz Merchant
Shalini Chopra

Chitra Subramanian
Manvi Dhillon
R. Jagannathan
Tavleen Singh

MASS COMMUNICATION

It is related to newspaper, magazine, book publishing, radio, television and film, these are items used for disseminating information to the public. This includes news-reading, reporting, anchoring, radio jockey, public-relations, advertising, production, web journalism, social media etc.

This is a growing field with high perks and salary. With proper education and experience, you may have a great future.

Eligibility: 10+2 /12th any stream
Courses:

- B.A. – Mass Communication
- B.B.A. – Mass Media Management
- M.A. – Communication & Journalism

Institutes/ Universities:

- AMU, Aligarh
- Anamalai University, Chennai
- JNU – New Delhi
- Symbiosis Institute of Mass Communication, Pune

Salary:
Starting salary for a Mass Communication is around INR. 2-4 lakhs per annum.
For more information you may visit the website below:
https://www.jagranjosh.com/institutes-colleges/journalism-mass-communication-coll

PUBLIC RELATIONS

Public relations focus on image building through best communication in the corporate and government sector. This also helps raise the value of corporate companies in the market and also increases value of shares in the market due to a strong image building. This is a growing field with high perks and salary. With proper education and experience, you may have a great future.

Eligibility: 10+2 /12th any stream
Courses:

- B.A. – Advertising & Public Relations
- M.A. - Advertising & Public Relations
- MBA

Institutes/ Universities:

IGNOU, Delhi   Indian Institute of Mass Communication, Delhi

JNU – New Delhi   Smt. Savitribai Phule University of Pune, Pune

Salary:
Starting salary for a Public Relations Manager is around INR. 3-4 lakhs per annum.
For more information you may visit the website below:
https://scoreindia.org/blog/best-institutes-of-public-relations-india/

Best Public Relations Consultants in India:

Ameer Ismail - Executive Director @ GolinOpinion
AmitMisra - Managing Director @ MSL Group

ART DIRECTION

This involves planning, creation, management and carrying out visual and images in newspapers, movies, magazines, etc.

Eligibility: 10+2 /12th any stream
Courses:

B.Sc   M.Sc

Institutes/ Universities:

Film & Television Institute of India (FTII), Pune

National School of Drama (NSD), Delhi

Satyajit Ray Film & Television Institute, Kolkata

St. Xavier College, Mumbai

Salary:
Starting salary for an Artist is around INR. 3-5 lakhs per annum.
For more information you may visit the website below:
http://www.zimainstitute.com/film-direction-courses.html

CHOREGRAPHY

This deals with carrying out dance in an innovative way, in which further to develop a new dance methodology. This gives an opportunity for expressing their new ideas with mindset.

Eligibility: 10+2 /12th any stream
Courses:

B.A in Dance   M.A in Dance

Institutes/ Universities:

BHU, Varanasi

Mumbai University

Sangeet Natak Academy, New Delhi

University of Mysore

Salary:

The average starting salary for choreographers varies from Rs 5-6 lakh per annum.

For more information you may visit the website below:

https://www.collegemagazine.com/the-10-best-colleges-for-aspiring-choreographers/

DIRECTION

Direction deals with creative aspects of production such as creating, shaping and controlling artistic and dramatic facets of a film or drama, visualization of script or screenplay, selection of sets or locations and special costume effects.

Eligibility: Bachelor's degree in any discipline

Courses:

B.A

M.A

Post Graduation Diploma

Institutes/ Universities:

Film & Television Institute of India (FTII), Pune

National School of Drama (NSD), Delhi

Salary:

The average starting salary is around Rs 4-5 lakh per annum.

For more information you may visit the website below:

https://www.quora.com/Which-is-the-best-film-school-in-india

Some of the National Award-Winning Directors in India

Adoor Gopalakrishnan

Aparna Sen

Ashutosh Gowarikar

Bala

Jayaraj

Sanjay Leela Bansali

Satyajit Ray

Rituparno Ghosh

FILM & DRAMA

It's linked with production of movies, tv serials, commercial advertisements, small serials, etc. It also involves sound system, camera management, etc.

Eligibility: 10+2/ 12th any stream

Courses:

- PG Diploma in Feature Film Screenplay Writing - 1 year
- PG Diploma in Film, Television & Digital Video Production
- PG Diploma in Feature Direction & Screenplay Writing - 3 year
- PG Graduate Certificate Course in TV Direction - 1 year

Institutes/ Universities:

- Film & Television Institute of India (FTII), Pune
- National School of Drama (NSD), Delhi
- Jawaharlal Nehru Architecture & Fine Arts University, Hyderabad
- Satyajit Ray Film & Television Institute, Kolkata

Salary:

Successful person can earn in lakhs & crores.
For more information you may visit the website below:
https://www.shiksha.com/mass-communication-media/film-tv/colleges/acting-colleges-india

PERFORMING ARTS

Eligibility: 10+2/ 12th any stream

Courses:

- Bachelor of Creative Arts (BCrA)
- Bachelor of Visual Arts (BVA)
- Bachelor of Fine Arts (BFA)
- Ph. D

Institutes/ Universities:

- BHU, Varanasi
- National School of Drama (NSD), Delhi
- Faculty of Fine Arts, Jamia Millia Islamia, New Delhi
- Delhi College of Arts, Delhi
- Satyajit Ray Film & Television Institute, Kolkata
- Film & Television Institute of India (FTII), Pune

Salary:
The salary varies depending on the job, a graduate in fine arts can start their career in between Rs 4-5 lakhs per annum.
For more information you may visit the website below:
https://targetstudy.com/colleges/bpa-performing-arts-degree-colleges-in-india.html
https://www.ftii.ac.in/p/admission

Famous Theatre Artists who are the Powerhouse Talent

Gitish Karnad   Makarand Deshpande

Nana Patekar   Naseeruddin Shah

Shabana Azmi   Shreeram Lagoo

Ratna Pathak Shah

VOCAL & INSTRUMENTAL

This involves music in films which includes composition of music, voice formation, singing of song, development of music for the success of films.

Eligibility: 10+2/ 12th any stream

Courses:

B.A Honours   M.A in Music

M.Phil   Ph. D

Institutes/ Universities:

Delhi University   Kurukshetra University

Mumbai University

Salary:
The salary of a Music Teacher is in between Rs 3-4 lakhs per annum.
For more information you may visit the website below:
https://www.coursesuggest.com/top-10-music-schools-colleges-india/

Some Best Indian Classical Musicians

Miyan Tamsen   M.S. Subbulakshmi

Ustad Ali Akbar Khan   Ustad Bismillah Khan

Ustad Zakir Hussain   Pandit Shiv Kumar Sharma

Pandit Hariprasad Chourasia

VISUAL ART, COMMUNICATION & ANIMATION

This is a very exciting field where everyone is interested to carry out work with their passion to develop a character. It is a growing field where there is a bright future for the students who want to make a career. It requires strong knowledge about computers and its use.

Eligibility: 10+2/ 12th any stream

Institutes/ Universities:

- Delhi University
- National Institute of Design, Ahmedabad-Gujarat
- St. Xavier's College, Kolkata-West Bengal
- Mumbai University
- National Institute of Film & Fine Arts, Kolkata-West Bengal

Salary:
Junior Animators or trainees could get between Rs 3-4 lakhs per annum.

https://collegedunia.com/courses/bachelor-of-fine-arts-bfa-animation-colleges-in-india

CINEMATOGRAPHY

This course is about fundamental tools of cinematography, animation and being able to work on various digital cameras. There is a bright career opportunity in the field of Cinematography.

Eligibility: 10+2/ 12th any stream

Courses:

- Bachelor of Film & Television Production
- PG Diploma in Film & Television
- Diploma in Cinematography

Institutes/ Universities:

- Film & Television Institute of India (FTII), Pune
- National Institute of Film & Fine Arts, Kolkata-West Bengal
- National Institute of Design, Ahmedabad-Gujarat
- St. Xavier's College, Kolkata-West Bengal

Salary:
In India, a cinematographer who has just joined the industry is paid around Rs 2-3 lakhs per annum.
For more information you may visit the website below:
https://collegedunia.com/courses/diploma-in-cinematography-colleges-in-india

COMMUNICATION DESIGN

This is specifically focused on brand building of the products which help to increase sales, revenue and increase presence in the market. This is now a very important thing for the companies to present in the market and to remain competitive.

Eligibility: 10+2/ 12th any stream
Courses:

B.A   *M.A*

Institutes/ Universities:
Indian Institute of Art & Design, Delhi

Salary:
Average starting salary is around Rs 3-5 lakhs per annum
For more information you may visit the website below:
https://www.graphic-design-institute.com/blogs/top-10-design-colleges-and-institutes-india

DESIGN

It is linked with various design formulations in the industry of textile, leather, fashion, gem, jewellery, clothing, ceramic, interior, Animation, film design, video programming, footwear design, accessories, furniture design.

Eligibility: 10+2/ 12th any stream

Courses:
Bachelor of Design   *Masters of Design*

Institutes/ Universities:

Delhi University   *Footwear Design & Development Institute*

IIT-Mumbai

National School of Design, Ahmedabad-Gujarat

National Institute of Fashion Technology, New Delhi

Salary:
Average starting salary is around Rs 4-5 lakhs per annum.
For more information you may visit the website below:
https://rathoredesign.com/top-design-colleges-in-india/

GRAPHIC DESIGNING

This is a combination of pictures, text, symbols through your visualization and artistic impression. It has a great future due to growing demand for animation.

Eligibility: 10+2/ 12th any stream
Institutes/ Universities:

BHU, Varanasi

IIT - Delhi

Mumbai University

National School of Design, Ahmedabad-Gujarat

Salary:
Average starting salary is around Rs 3-5 lakhs per annum.
For more information you may visit the website below:
https://www.collegedekho.com/design/graphic_design_illustration-colleges-in-india/

PHOTOGRAPHY

This sector has specialized areas like Commercial photography, Scientific photography, Business photography, Wildlife photography, Fashion photography, Industrial photography, Press Photography, and portrait work, etc. This link with taking images of public, individual, area which is utilized for various purposes.

Eligibility: 10+2/ 12th any stream

Courses:

Bachelor of Fine Arts

Masters of Fine Arts

Institutes/ Universities:

College of Arts, Delhi *IGNOU, Delhi*
National Institute of
Photography, Mumbai

Salary:

As per India Today Magazine a photographer can earn around Rs 2-3.5 lakhs per annum.

For more information you may visit the website below: https://www.shiksha.com/arts-fine-visual-performing/photography/articles/top-10-colleges-for-photography-courses-in-india-blogId-11445

Some Best Indian Photographers

Atul Kasbekar *Arjun Mark*
Dabboo Ratnani *Dayanita Singh*
Prabuddha Dasgupta *Raghu Rai*
Rathika Ramasamy *Sooni Taraporewala*

ACTUARIAL SCIENCE

This science deals with the interlinking of finance, economics, computer knowledge, maths, etc. for the application to get probable output. This applies to measure risk involved in various industries like financial sectors, business sectors and other sectors. It is in utmost demand for the growing finance sector.

Eligibility: 10+2/ 12th any stream

Courses:

International PG Diploma in *International PG Diploma in Risk*
General Insurance (IPGDGI) *Management (IPGDRM)*
PG Diploma in Actuarial Sciences

Institutes/ Universities:

Institute of Actuaries of India, Mumbai *VNS Gujarat University, Surat*

Salary:

The salary of experienced actuaries is much more. Actuarial students can expect to start their career with an annual package of anywhere between Rs. 4 to 5 lakhs.

For more information you may visit the website below:

https://collegedunia.com/courses/bachelor-of-science-bsc-actuarial-science-colleges-in-india

BANK MANAGEMENT

This is a very demanding sector which has super specialize areas like finance, investment, retail, rural banking, agricultural banking, etc. are existing in this sector. This involves providing loans to Government, Corporate, Citizens at the proper rate to manage financial activities. It also involves raising funds through issuing bonds.

Eligibility: 10+2/ 12th with accounting

Institutes/ Universities:

Annamalai University, Tamil Nadu	Bangalore University
IGNOU, Delhi	Mumbai University

Salary:
Average starting salary is around Rs 8-10 lakhs per annum.
For more information you may visit the website below: http://www.nibmindia.org/

BUSINESS ADMINISTRATION

This deals with the best management practices for the public and resources, achieving targeted physical & financial goals of the organization. It is a demanding sector in industry by the young generation.

Eligibility: 10+2/ 12th in any stream

Courses:

BBA	MBA

Institutes/ Universities:

College of Symbiosis, Pune	Faculty of Management Studies, Delhi University
IGNOU, Delhi	Institute of Management (IIM) – Ahmedabad, Lucknow, Bangalore

Salary:
The average salary of a Business Administrator is Rs 5-10 lakhs per annum.

For more information you may visit the website below:
https://www.jagranjosh.com/institutes-colleges/business-management-colleges

CHARTED ACCOUNTANCY

It has a key role in formulation of financial policies & investment plans of a company, and to make business plans for sustainable growth of a company. This makes a difference in management of the company in respect of finance.

Eligibility: Commerce graduate with 50% or non-commerce with 60% or passed candidate of CA foundation course.

Admission Process:

The applications are invited one year in advance for these courses. The examinations are held twice a year, May & November.

- Enrolment for the CA Foundation Course are 10+2 / 12th Std
- Enrolment for Intermediate Course (graduates can join directly)
- Register as an Articled Clerk with a practising CA for undergoing practical training, student with Board of Studies - ICAI for theoretical education

Courses:

CA – Foundation Course   *CA – Intermediate Course*

Institutes/ Universities:

The Institute of charted Accountants of India, New Delhi

Salary:

The average salary of Chartered Accountants in India ranges from 6-7 lakhs to 30 lakhs. International packages are even higher ranging up to 75 lakhs. Last year stats showed that the average salary of CAs in India was offered around 7.36 lakhs p.a. in the campus placement conducted by ICAI.

For more information you may visit the website below:
https://www.collegedekho.com/ca-colleges-in-india/

CERTIFIED FINANCIAL ADVISOR – CFA

This gives an insight in corporate finance, financial management, investment management and financial services of the organization. It has three levels like Preliminary; inter and final level. It is recognized as a Postgraduate Diploma in Financial Analysis by AICTE. It is a self-study programme in which the Institute supplies study material to the enrolled students. This has two courses like Diploma in Basic Finance (DBF) and Merchant Banking and Financial Services (MBFS).

Eligibility: Any graduate

The candidates who qualify in the admission test and those who are exempted from passing the admission test are enrolled for the Programme. In this, a student is allowed a maximum period of three years to complete the preliminary level of the programme and a maximum period of seven years to complete the entire programme.
Exemptions: Candidates who are MBA's, CA, CWA, CS, First Class Graduated, PG, Executive with 10 years of experience.

Programmes:
- Regular CFA Program
- Graduates from any discipline, students appearing in final year
- Accelerated CFA Program
- First Class Graduates, PG's, working professionals like CA, CWA, CS, MBA, CAIIB
- CFA Foundation Course
- Degree college student interested in pursuing prof. certification like CFA Program

Admission Process:
The admission to both the programs is through a basic test. The admission test aims at testing the aptitude of the candidates for professional studies in financial analysis. Hence the quantitative reasoning ability of the candidate is tested. The admission test is held four times in a year in the months of January, April, July and October.

Salary:
The average pay scale of these professionals proposed to be Rs 3-4 lakh per annum and the highest salary that a CFA can draw lies close to Rs 20 lakh.

For more information you may visit the website below:
https://collegedunia.com/courses/cfa-chartered-financial-analyst-colleges-in-india

EVENT MANAGEMENT

This has growing demand in India due to the rising economic power of India. An Event is a program, function, seminar, exhibition, show, award ceremony, marriage or even family party. The activities and assignments in event management involve event marketing, Costs and Budgets available, advertisements, reviews, demos etc.

Eligibility: 10+2 /12th with good knowledge of English

Courses:

Certificate Course in Event Management (CEM)

Diploma in in Event Management (DEM)

Graduate Program in Event Management

Institutes/ Universities:

IGNOU, New Delhi

Mumbai University

National Institute of Event Management, Mumbai

Salary:
Salary of an Event Planner is around Rs 3-5 lakhs per annum.

For more information you may visit the website below:
https://www.collegedekho.com/hospitality-aviation/event_management_2-colleges-in-india/

HOSPITAL MANAGEMENT

This has great career prospects due to the rising image of India as a medical tourism industry. It is also due to the low cost of medical treatment in India. Hospital Management is related to various aspects such as purchase of equipment, human resource, and promotion of health services, economic planning, and budget allocation for hospital services.

Eligibility: 10+2 /12th any stream

Courses:

Bachelor of Hospital Management (BHA)
Masters of Hospital Management (MHA)
M.Phil-Hospital & Health Management Systems
Ph.D Programme in Health Services Management

Institutes/ Universities:

AIIMS, New Delhi
Armed Forces Medical College, Pune
BITS, Pilani-Rajasthan
Devi Ahilya Vishwavidyalaya, Indore
Punjab University
Tata Institute of Social Sciences, Mumbai

Salary:
Salary is around Rs 5-7 lakhs per annum.
For more information you may visit the website below:
https://collegedunia.com/courses/bachelor-of-hospital-management-bhm-colleges-in-india

HOTEL MANAGEMENT

Hotel Management is in demand due to the rise of tourism in our country. This involves all activities like housekeeping, beverage, catering and other services. This also involves event management. Hence event management also included here.

Eligibility: 10+2 /12th any stream

Courses:

Bachelor in Hotel Management
M.Sc in Hospitality Administration
PG Diploma in Accommodation, Operations & Management

Institutes/ Universities:

Delhi Institute of Hotel Management, New Delhi
Delhi Institute of Hotel Management, New Delhi

National Council for Hotel Management & Catering Technology, New Delhi

National Council for Hotel Management & Catering Technology, New Delhi

Salary:
Salary is around Rs 3-5 lakhs per annum.
For more information you may visit the website below:
https://collegedunia.com/courses/diploma-in-event-management-colleges-in-india

HUMAN RESOURCE MANAGEMENT

This is the heart of the organization where the right people need to be recruited to run the company. Better the people, more are chances of the organization running successfully.

HR deals with proper organization and management staff in the organization. It is responsible for proper manpower planning. It starts from selection, assessment, training and appointment along with settlement after retirement. It also focuses on the Union and administration relationship, labour relationship with the system, staff welfare, merger and acquisition strategy during takeover from other companies.

Eligibility: 10+2 /12th any stream or a graduate

Courses:

Bachelor of Business Administration in Human Resource Management

Master of Bachelor of Business Administration in Human Resource Management

Master of Bachelor of Business Administration in Human Resource Management

Executive Diploma Programme in Human Resource Management

Institutes/ Universities:

Indian Institute of Social Welfare & Business Management, West Bengal

IGNOU, Delhi

Smt. Savitribai Phule University of Pune, Pune

Indian Institute of Management (IIM)- Ahmedabad, Kolkata, Bangalore

Jamnalal Bajaj College of Management, Mumbai

Salary:
Salary is around Rs 6-10 lakhs per annum.
For more information you may visit the website below:
https://collegedunia.com/mba/human-resources-management-colleges

INSURANCE

It is the most advanced and growing sector in India due to raised awareness among the public for the better future of the family members. India has a great future for insurance as we have 4% of the population who are insured. Hence still there is huge scope for the growth of the insurance industry.

This is like which relates to the present as well as future. Now various insurance products like Term Insurance, Health Insurance, ULIP scheme came in the market for the customers.

Eligibility: 10+2 /12th any stream or a graduate

Courses:

B. Com *M. Com*
MBA

Institutes/ Universities:

IGNOU, Delhi *Mumbai University*
Smt. Savitribai Phule University of Pune, Pune *The Insurance Institute of India, Mumbai*

Different Types of Insurance Policies in India:
- Term Plan-Pure Risk Cover
- Unit Linked Insurance Plan (ULIP) – Insurance + Investment
- Endowment Plan-Insurance + Savings
- Money Back-Periodic returns with insurance cover
- Whole Life Insurance-Life coverage to the life assured

Salary:
Salary is around Rs 4-5 lakhs per annum.
For more information you may visit the website below:
https://collegedunia.com/mba/insurance-colleges

BACHELOR OF EDUCATION – B. ED

This sector focuses on training teachers for teaching at primary, secondary and senior secondary students.

Eligibility: Graduate in any stream

Courses:

B. Ed M. Ed
Ph.D

Institutes/ Universities:

BHU, Varanasi Delhi University
IGNOU, Delhi IGNOU, Delhi
Smt. Savitribai Phule University of Pune, Pune

Salary:
Salary is around Rs 3-5 lakhs per annum.
For more information you may visit the website below: https://www.collegedekho.com/bed-colleges-in-india/

CORPORATE INTELLIGENCE – DETECTIVE

It takes the proper information on the present condition and other situation of the corporate companies to avoid any future problem. This has been carried out with the help of insider staff for the concrete information. This is one of the important things for any person who is linked with doing investment in the company or going for joint ventures or acquiring the new companies. Hence it helps in making decisions in the organization.

For this purpose, detectives are utilized in an efficient manner. These are always private people.

Eligibility: 10+2 /12th any stream

Courses:

Private Detective Course to become a Private Detective

Various modules courses need to pass for Corporate Intelligence Examination

Salary:
Salary is around Rs 5-6 lakhs per annum.
For more information you may visit the website below:
http://www.ifsindia.com/
https://economictimes.indiatimes.com/industry/services/education/detectives-plan-to-set-up-intelligence-institute-in-delhi/articleshow/312752.cms?from=mdr

INTERIOR DESIGNING

Interior designing is the art of designing interior, furniture, furnishings, design patterns, colour combinations to meet the demand of customized solutions.

Eligibility: 10+2 /12th any stream

Courses:

Bachelor of Design - Interior Design   *B. Sc – Interior Design*
M. Sc – Interior Design   *Bachelor of Interior Design (BID)*

Institutes / Universities:

Institute of Design & Media, Mumbai   *Mumbai University*
Pearl Academy, Mumbai   *Raffles Design International, Mumbai*

Salary:
Salary is around Rs 3-4 lakhs per annum.
For more information you may visit the website below:
https://collegedunia.com/design/interior-design/maharashtra-colleges

LIBRARY SCIENCE

It deals with the study of management, maintaining and preserving records, books, newspaper and information.

Eligibility: 10+2 /12th any stream

Courses:

Bachelor in Library & Information Sciences (BLISc)   *Masters in Library & Information Sciences (MLISc)*
Masters in Library Science (MLSc)

Institutes / Universities:

Medical Library Association of India (MLAI) Delhi University

Salary:

Salary is around Rs 2-2.5 lakhs per annum.

For more information you may visit the website below: https://targetstudy.com/colleges/blibsc-degree-colleges-in-india.html

NUTRITION & DIETETICS

This is one of the fastest growing areas of the healthcare industry where it mainly focuses on the promotion of good health, goods food practices, guiding right food for the health of particular people. This becomes a necessity of today's scenario where everybody is moving under pressure and not having time for personal health.

Eligibility: 10+2 /12th with PCB

Courses:

B.Sc in Food & Nutrition

M.Sc in Home Science - Food Science & Nutrition

Diploma in Dietetics

PG Diploma in Food & Nutrition

Institutes / Universities:

IGNOU, Delhi

National Institute of Nutrition, Hyderabad

SNDT Women's University, Mumbai

Mumbai University

Smt. Savitribai Phule University of Pune, Pune

Salary:

Salary is around Rs 3-5 lakhs per annum.

For more information you may visit the website below: https://www.collegedekho.com/para-medical/nutrition_and_dietetics-colleges-in-india/

CAREER IN POLITICS

Now to make a career in politics, there are courses started after graduation where you are trained in Constitution and Indian politics. You are trained and groomed along with big politicians and given a chance to see their work style and accordingly you also understand how to groom yourself.

Prospectus- If you really want to make a career, then this is the best way to enter and understand how government and politics go hand-in-hand to run it. This course will give you bright exposure

Eligibility: Graduation in any field
Courses:

M.A in Political Leadership & Government

PG Diploma in Political Leadership (PGDPL)

Institutes / Universities:

MIT School of Government, Pune

Rajiv Gandhi National Institute of Youth Development

Salary:
Salary in the field of politics depends upon your designation and post. In India, MLA receives an annual salary of 6 lacs. The MLA daily allowance for each day of attending assembly is Rs. 2000.
For more information you may visit the website below:
http://www.mitsog.org/
http://www.rgniyd.gov.in/

RESEARCH SCIENTIST

This is one of the best careers for one who has inclination towards research. Whoever has a good education background and has an ability to apply knowledge in practical fields.

Prospectus- If candidate have Ph.D. from recognized institution from abroad and recognized from Indian Institution. They have better prospectus to get hired and get good incentives.

Most important thing to have interest and commitment in work. Then this would be a great career where one really enjoys life by giving his full time. This is a great career, but it is highly neglected in India but has great demand in developed nations due to high status and huge salary.

Why so much difference- In USA & European nations, Teachers, Professors, scientists, Professor Emeritus have greater status and earning than doctors, engineers, lawyers, etc. They have flexible hours, freedom to work from home, have two-month time in a year when they can do independent consulting whose income would be extra along with their regular salary. For abroad master and doctoral programmes require to clear the GRE & TOEFL Exam.

Eligibility: PG Degree, Ph. D
Courses:
Research Program in various fields
Institutes / Universities:

AIIMS, New Delhi	*Columbia University, NewYork-USA*
Boston University	*Georgia Tech. University, Atlanta-USA*
London School of Economics, London	*Oxford University*
Massachusetts Institute of Technology, USA	*National University of Singapore*
PUSA, New Delhi	*IIT-Mumbai, Kolkata, Delhi*
Indian Institute of Science	*ISRO, Chennai*
JNU, New Delhi	*Smt. Savitribai Phule University of Pune*

For more information you may visit the website below:
http://www.iitd.ac.in/
http://www.cornell.edu/
http://www.lse.ac.uk/
http://www.columbia.edu/

INTERESTING CAREER FOR INTERESTING STUDENTS

ALCOHOL TECHNOLOGY

As fascinating as this course sounds, it doesn't call for quite as much debauchery as the name suggests. And even though it doesn't entail chugging liquor for a practical exam, it's really unique, nonetheless. Vasant dada Sugar Institute (VSI) is an autonomous body that was established in 1975 by sugarcane growers of cooperative sugar factories in the state of Maharashtra.

Under one umbrella, they carry out all scientific, technical and educational functions relevant to the sugar industry, and they also have a Department of Alcohol Technology that has been working towards helping the distillery industry.

Their main work involves perfecting the ways in which they can increase the productivity of this industry, mainly by developing and adopting better technology.

The department offers three types of courses – regular, short-term and national-level workshops and seminars that will equip students to undertake research for developing cost-effective alcohol production technologies from alternate raw materials.

Eligibility: 10+2/ 12th with PCM and 45%

Institutes:
Vasant dada Sugar Institute, Maharashtra

ASTRO-BIOLOGY

Astrobiology is an interdisciplinary field. If you want to become an astro-biologist, first you have to do your B.Sc in any of the following fields based on your interest.

- Microbiology
- Geology
- Biology
- Botany
- Biotechnology
- Physics
- Chemistry
- zoology
- Astrophysics
- Astronomy
- Oceanology

Read astrobiology-related scientific journals, which will help you to make your career better. In IARC, you can get short time courses based on Astrobiology.

NASA also provides astrobiology courses:

- Space sciences Astrobiology- Florida Institute of technology
- Astrobiology minor program- Pennsylvania state university
- A certificate program in planets and life- Princeton University
- Astrobiology minor- Rensselaer polytechnic institute
- An undergraduate minor in astrobiology- University of

Arizona

University: Indian Astrobiology Research Centre, Mumbai Every child, at some point of time growing up, has dreamed of being an astronaut. And for some, Mumbai's Indian Astrobiology Research Centre (IARC) is keeping that dream alive. Astrobiology is the study of the origin, evolution and distribution of life in the universe, and even probes into the possibility of extra-terrestrial life.

The IARC is an autonomous scientific body that conducts and encourages theoretical research in the field, and they also offer education and outreach initiative-related opportunities, such as externships, volunteer-ship and freelance opportunities. And if your space-thirst still isn't quenched, they even have a diploma course in other fields of study such as Astronomy & Cosmology, Space Sciences and Evolution.

For more information you may visit the website below: http://entrance-exam.net/procedure-to-become-an-astrobiologist/

FISHERY

Before the name of this course makes you jump to conclusions, let's start off with a disclaimer; this course does not teach people how to fish, however great that would be.

The Tamil Nadu Fisheries University (TNFU) was set up by Tamil Nadu Fisheries Industry owing to the importance of the fisheries sector in the Indian economy.

It focuses on aquaculture-based studies, such as adopting scientific methods to harness maximum benefit with minimum input without harming the environment or exhausting natural resources.

Their courses also teach students the process involved in scientific rearing of tilapia, catfish, shrimps, loaches and other ornamental fish.

To top it up, they even work towards diagnosing fish diseases and testing the quality of fishery products, thereby working towards increasing productivity and sustainability of livelihood.

Eligibility: 10+2 /12th with PCB and 50%
Admission Process: LPU-NEST, AUCET, GPAT, JEE
Institute: Tamil Nadu Fisheries University
Tamil Nadu Fisheries University

FOOD FLAVORIST / FOOD CHEMIST

Candidates who want to become a food flavorist should pursue B.Sc or M.Sc in chemistry . You can take your undergraduate degree in chemistry or biology and then go for a master's degree in food science program.

If you want to become a food flavorist or food chemisist then you should have a good sense of taste and smell. If you enjoyed balancing equations and forming covalent bonds while you were in school, a food flavorist might be the path for you.

Trust us, it is a legitimate profession. The Indian Institute of Hospitality & Management (IIHM) in Mumbai & the SRM University offers a course that helps people understand fragrances and flavours to products, to enhance its taste and smell.

The job basically requires mixing various ingredients to create unique flavours, which essentially means that you need to gain a thorough understanding of aroma chemicals, essential oils, plant extracts and other similar aromatic ingredients.

Eligibility: 10+2 /12th with PCB and 50% or a Graduate in any stream
Institutes:
Indian Institute of Hospitality & Management
SRM Department of Food Process Engineering, Ghaziabad-UP.

Salary: Salary in this field is based mainly on experience and the ability to blend flavors. A fresher in the industry can expect around Rs. 15,000-25,000/- per month. However, one with experience & a reputation in the field can earn even lakhs through this profession.

"Don't Let Schooling Interfere with Your Education"

GARDENING PROGRAMME

This sector deals with Nursery, Flowering plants & Farmhouse Management leaning towards horticulture, Garden Craft and aesthetics. There are short term courses run by the Centre for Extra Mural Studies of Mumbai University, which helps to understand the nuances of growing different varieties of plants and the best suitable conditions for them.

Eligibility: 10+2 /12th or a Graduate in any stream

Program/Courses:
Nursery   Farm House Management
Garden Craft Course

Institute:
Centre for Extra-Mural Studies of Mumbai University

MOUNTAINEERING

This is one of the exciting career options and being a part of an adventurous journey ahead. Though no special training is necessary to join the courses, the students are advised to do jogging and long walks.

Age Limit:

Mountaineering/ Water Rafting of Paragliding	18 to 40 yrs
Adhoc Adventure/ Adventure	12 to 55 yrs
Senior Citizen (Adhoc Adventure)	60 yrs above
Skiing	10 to 60 yrs

Institutes/ Universities:

ITBP Training, Auli	Jawahar Institute of Mountaineering (JIM), Pahalgam
Himalayan Mountaineering Institute (HMI), Darjeeling	National Institute of Mountaineering
Nehru Institute of Mountaineering (NIM), Uttarkashi	

For all those pumped with adrenaline at just the thought of trekking, rock climbing and other similar activities, enrol yourself in the mountaineering institute as given above.

There are mainly two levels of training – basic and advanced – and after completing these two phases, you can go on to become an instructor, or you can take up a career in mountaineering and allied sports.

PET GROOMING

There are no strict formal education requirements for becoming a dog groomer; however, employers usually prefer candidates with a high school diploma or equivalent. Most of the groomers acquire training through apprenticeship programs, which typically last 6-10 weeks.

This fascinating course is hand-crafted and designed specifically for all animal lovers and enthusiasts. While it is still a relatively new career option in India, the concept of pet grooming 186 is slowly gaining popularity. The job essentially deals with the hygiene and appearance of pets mainly cats, dogs and horses.

Institutes/ Universities:
Whiskers & Tails Franchise – Pet Grooming Academy, Mumbai

Salary:
In India the salary of a pet groomer is anywhere between Rs 1-2.5 lakhs per annum.

PUBLIC HEALTH ENTOMOLOGY

There are many insects that have a huge impact on human health, such as malaria-causing mosquitoes. These insects carry vectors which are harmful for humans. Public Health Entomology involves researching the behavioural pattern and ecology of various species that affect human health, and thereby aiding the resolution of these issues. The need for such skilled technicians arises mainly because of the climbing death tolls as an aftermath of diseases like malaria and dengue, to name a few, and more knowledge of this field can fuel better-informed treatment.

Eligibility for Admission:
B.Sc, MBBS, B.E, B.Tech degree with biotechnology as one of the subjects shall be permitted to appear and qualify for the M.Sc. Public

Health Entomology degree examination in non-clinical subjects under the School of Medical Sciences after a course of study of two academic years.

Institutes/ Universities:
Guru Gobind Singh Indraprastha University, Delhi
Vector Control Research Centre (VCRC), Pondicherry University

Salary:
An entry level entomologist with 1-3 years of experience earns an average salary of Rs 4-5 lakhs per annum.

SPA MANAGEMENT

Every single person, at some point or the other, has experienced stress, which can lead to various serious health-related problems if it escalates.

Spas are the heaven that relieves that stress, and helps you relax your mind and body, and causing that kind of peace for another person is an art that can be learnt.

A spa management training institute will teach you all that you need to know, in terms of being a good masseuse as well as helping prospective owners and developers understand the business.

The basic fee for the B.Sc in Beauty Cosmetology course in India may range from INR 5,000 to 10 lacs, for the duration of 3 years. Such applicants are hired as Sales Manager, Hair Stylist, Teacher & Lecturer, Manicurist, Beauty Consultant, Brand Manager, Cosmetics Business Development Manager, Spa Therapist, Nail Artist etc. The average compensation of a Cosmetologist can be between 2 lacs to 8 lakhs every year.

Institutes/ Universities:
Orient SPA Academy
Ananda SPA Institute

TEA TASTING

The world of tea is a fascinating one and goes way beyond teabags in boxes on supermarket shelves, which is the only encounter most people have.

There's a particular art involved in appreciating good tea, and this art is one that can be learnt, developed and nurtured. Working as a tea sommelier involves more than just tasting tea.

It requires you to understand and perceive the quality, give advice on methods of improvement, branding, all of which requires a good knowledge of cultivation and manufacturing.

Eligibility: Graduation in Botany, Food Sciences, Horticulture or allied fields. Tea tasters should also have initiative and be knowledgeable about the tea market and be alerted to changing market forces, and should be willing to undertake strenuous work.

A certificate course is offered to understand the tea tasting techniques. The courses span from 3 months certificate course to 1 year diploma. Salaries are good and even a trainee earns 5000/month. After completion of training, one can earn 20,000-30,000/ month.

Institutes/ Universities:
Birla Institute of Futuristic Studies
Dipras Institute of Professional Studies
Indian Institute of Plantation Management, Bangalore

"Education is for improving the lives of others and for leaving your community and world better than you found it."
-Marian Wright Eddman

"I believe that education is all about being something. Seeing passion and enthusiasm helps push an educational message."
-Steve Irwin

EXCELLENT CAREER IDEAS FOR LANGUAGE LEARNERS

Learning foreign languages not only strengthens better understanding of cultures, perspectives employability but also improves cognitive skills, concentration span, memorisation and multi-tasking skills in an individual.

Eligibility: 10th /10+2 for Diploma & Certificate courses. 10+2 with Diploma or Certificate courses for B.A. The eligibility criteria are also varied for M.A among the universities & language centres.

Courses: There are a variety of short & long duration courses to learn languages like Japanese, Italian, German, Russian, Chinese, Portuguese, Spanish, Persian, Arabic and French.

Short term (2months-1 year): Certificate / Diploma / Advance Diploma Courses

Long term (2years-3years): Bachelor's Degree & PG Diploma Courses

Master's degree (1 or 2 year): M.Phil, MA, Ph.D, etc.

5-year Integrated Master's course

Institutes/ Universities:

Central Institute of English & Foreign Languages, Hyderabad

Aligarh Muslim University, Aligarh

Banaras Hindu University, Varanasi

IGNOU, New Delhi

Jamia Millia Islamia, New Delhi.

Barkatullah Vishwa Vidyalaya, Bhopal

Madurai Kamaraj University, Madurai

DO YOU WANT A CAREER IN FOREIGN LANGUAGE?

This is going to become a huge area of employment in the future for India due to the working of Multinational Companies in India. This helped to increase demand for people who are having knowledge of foreign languages. Also, there are opportunities in India and abroad, as follows:

- **Become a translator**
  Believe it or not, translation skills are not the same thing as foreign language skills. You can be amazingly fluent in a language and yet still be a useless translator.

- **Get a career as an interpreter**
  Translating and interpreting are two totally different

things. Translation is about the written word – changing texts. Interpreting is spoken and (I would argue) a much more challenging job than translation.

This is because you must deal with people who are speaking spontaneously and colloquially, and you need to be equally spontaneous and accurate!

This is very challenging as well as a rewarding job if you like it.

- **Apply for a foreign language intelligence role**
  So even though foreign languages may be your forte, people skills and personal charisma could be the determining factor for whether a typical intelligence officer role is worth going for.
- **Work as a teacher**
  This is a good option for a career, provided you have interest in teaching.
- **Work in a customer service industry**
  While not a foreign language job per se, this is worth mentioning. Customer service roles of just about every kind are increasingly in need of more multilingual staff.
- **Linguist job in the military**
  This is a very challenging job in respect of responsibility and has great respect.

  Now the important thing is to learn how you can increase your value in the job market. Which language should you learn?

WHICH FOREIGN LANGUAGE TO LEARN IN INDIA?

It is very difficult to decide which language you should learn with respect to a good career. In this, it depends on your liking, future goal, where you want to settle, remuneration, back support, guidance, etc.

By considering these things, you can see popular language and their benefit on which you can take further decision

Top Foreign Languages to Learn in India

French (Français)
Spanish (Español)
Mandarin Chinese (普通话 / Pǔtōnghuà)
Portuguese (Português)
German (Deutsch)
Japanese (日本語 / Nihongo)
Russian (русский / Rússkiy)

Most Widely Spoken Foreign Languages.
Top 4 foreign languages with the most speakers (Natives and Non-Natives) are **Mandarin Chinese**, **Spanish**, **Arabic**, and **French**.

- **French (Français)**
  French is the most popular foreign language to learn in India. Since French is the part of most School and College curriculum, more than 1 lakh students are studying French in Delhi / NCR only.
  French is also one of the best foreign languages to learn for jobs in corporate sectors in India. Many multinational companies use French as their working language in a wide range of activities.

- **German (Deutsch)**
  Even though German is not widely spoken, such as French, Spanish, Arabic, or Chinese. It is still the second most popular foreign language in India after French. The five main reasons: The most spoken mother tongue in Europe. It is the official language in Germany, Austria, Switzerland, and more. Germany is an economic powerhouse. And the ability to speak German offers plenty of job opportunities in many big German companies.

- **Spanish (Español)**
  With 20 Spanish-speaking countries, it is one of the most widely spoken languages in the world. Spanish language in India is the third most popular foreign language to learn after French and German.

- **Japanese (日本語 / Nihongo)**
  Demand for the Japanese language is high due to growing India-Japan relations and Japanese companies expanding Indian operations. Japan is synonymous with high quality and technologically

advanced products. Japanese is the most popular choice among East Asian languages in India. This is difficult to learn. Hence it is highly paid.

- **Mandarin Chinese (普通话 / Pǔtōnghuà)**
  More than a billion people speak Mandarin Chinese in the world. The 21st century belongs to China, and knowing the Chinese language will allow you to compete effectively in the global economy of the future. China has become an enormous market, and international businesses and companies are looking for people who can talk in Chinese and operate successfully in China's cultural context.

- **Russian (русский / Rússkiy)**
  The Russian language has been popular in India for a very long time. However, the demand has declined in the last decade or so. It is spoken by over 300 million people around the world. It is the most geographically widespread language of Eurasia and the largest native language in Europe. 7. Italian (Italiano) Italian is the eighth largest economy and ranks as one of the wealthiest countries in the world. Italian is the most romantic of the romance languages. Several International Italian companies like Banco, Fiat, Benetton, Gucci, Lloyd, Ferrari, Marconi, and Pinnacle that have set up their businesses in India are looking for those who are proficient in the Italian language in India.

"If you want to learn, whatever your reason – as long as you have a purpose – you're more likely to reach your language goals …"

Best Institutes to Learn Foreign Language in India

AMU, Aligarh	*BHU, Varanasi*
Delhi University	*Jamia Millia Islamia University*
JNU, New Delhi	*Smt. Savitribai Phule University of Pune, Pune*
University of Calcutta	

TRAVEL & TOURISM

It is a fastly growing industry in India. This has a fascinating career due to a wide range of opportunities to travel to different countries and places. Hence those who have interest to move from one place to another place this is the best career option for them.

Eligibility: 10+2/ 12th in any stream

Courses:

- Bachelor in Tourism
- Diploma in Tourism Management
- Diploma in International Airline & Travel Management
- Masters in Tourism

Institutes:

- Delhi University
- Pondicherry University, Pondicherry
- Mumbai University, Mumbai
- Indian Institute of Travel & Tourism Management, New Delhi
- IGNOU, New Delhi

Salary:

Salary is around Rs 4-5 lakhs per annum.

For more information you may visit the website below: https://bschool.careers360.com/colleges/list-of-tourism-colleges-in-india

SPORTS & SPORTS MANAGEMENT

This is specially related with the games, management of physical activities, team work, professional learning of the games and management of competition. This provides competitive management of games and sports competition.

Eligibility: 10+2/ 12th in any stream

Courses:

- Diploma in Sports Science & Nutrition
- B.Sc in Physical Education, Health Education & Sports Science
- B.A in Sports Management
- BBA in Sports Management

Institutes:

- Delhi University
- Smt. Savitribai Phule University of Pune, Pune

Indira Gandhi Institute of Physical Education & Sports Science, New Delhi

SNDT Women's University, Mumbai

National Institute of Sports, Patiala

SPORTS & PHYSICAL EDUCATION

This is an education which focuses on sports, physical fitness, development of the physical structure of a person and learning of taking care of self and a sports person.

Eligibility: 10+2/ 12th in any stream

Courses:

Bachelor in Physical Education   Masters in Physical Education
Ph.D

Institutes:

Andhra University, Visakhapatnam	BHU, Varanasi
College of Physical Education, Pune	Indira Gandhi Institute of Physical Education & Sports Science, New Delhi
North Eastern Hill University, Shillong	University of Mysore, Mysuru
Smt. Savitribai Phule University of Pune, Pune	University of Rajasthan, Jaipur
IGNOU, New Delhi	Delhi University

For more information you may visit the website below: https://www.careerindia.com/top-10-colleges-physical-education-india-011970.html

What are the job roles for Physical Education?

- Teacher
- Assistant Professor
- Sports Manager
- Physical Therapist
- Physical Education
- Trainer
- Health Educator Coach
- Fitness Instructor
- Sports Journalist

Top Colleges/ Universities abroad offering Physical Education

- Arizona State University

- The University of Texas at Austin
- Texas A&M University
- University of Arizona
- California State University - Long Beach

CAREER IN SUPER SPORTS

Professional sports as opposed to amateur sports in which athletes receive payment for their performance. Professional athleticism has come to the fore through a combination of developments. Mass Media and increased leisure have brought larger audiences, so that sports organizations or teams can command large incomes.

As a result, more sports people can afford to make athleticism their primary career, devoting the training time necessary to increase skills, physical condition, and experience to modern levels of achievement. This proficiency has also helped boost the popularity of sports. Most sports played professionally also have amateur players far outnumbering the professionals.

CRICKET

A Cricket player involves extensive travelling to play matches abroad. Cricketers can spend as many as six months playing various international series or tournaments. There are a number of perks that come along with a career in cricket.

Becoming a Professional Cricket Player - Play for a Club. In order to become a professional player, you must have an experience playing for a Cricket Club. Find a way to Stand out. A valuable player is good in many different roles.

FOOTBALL

Football is a family of team sports that involve, to varying degrees, kicking a ball to score a goal. Unqualified, the word football normally means the form of football that is the most popular where the word is used. Sports commonly called football include Association Football (known as soccer in some countries); Gridiron football (specifically American Football or Canadian Football); Australian rules football; Rugby Football (either Rugby League or

Rugby Union); and Gaelic Football. These various forms of football are known as football codes.

Popular Football academies in India:
- Premier Indian Football Academy (PIFA)
- TATA Football Academy (TFA)
- All India Football Federation (AIFF)

VOLLYBALL

Volleyball is a team sport in which two teams of six players are separated by a net. Each team tries to score points by grounding a ball on the other team's court under organized rules. It has been a part of the official program of the Summer Olympic Games since Tokyo 1964. The complete set of rules are extensive, but play essentially proceeds as follows: a player on one of the teams begins a 'rally' by serving the ball (tossing or releasing it and then hitting it with a hand or arm), from behind the back boundary line of the court, over the net, and into the receiving team's court.

Volleyball is a sport played all over India, both in rural as well as urban India. It is a popular recreation sport. India was ranked 5th in Asia, and 27th in the world in 2013. Doing well in the youth and junior levels, India came in second in the 2003 World Youth Championships. Currently, a major problem for the sport is the lack of sponsors.

BADMINTON

Indian shuttlers Saina Nehwal, K. Srikanth and P.V. Sindhu are ranked amongst top-10 in current BWF ranking. Prakash Padukone was the first player from India to achieve world no.1 spot in the game and after him K. Srikanth made it to the top spot as male player for the second time in April 2018 and Saina Nehwal is the first female player from India to achieve World no.1 spot in April 2015. The most successful doubles player from India is

Jwala Gutta, who is the only Indian to have been ranked in the top-10 of two categories.
For more information you may visit the website below:
https://www.univariety.com/search/india/top-sports-colleges

INDIAN RAILAY SERVICE

Indian Railway is the largest railway network in India, second largest network in the World and largest employer in India with 1.3 million staff. It has 11 departments with more than 400 cadres of staff with huge complexity. There are a number of ways through which officers and staff get recruited. This is explained in the following way:

Officers are Recruited through:

UNION PUBLIC SERVICE COMMISSION

There are three exams conducted by UPSC in which 4 services come from CIVIL SERVICES EXAM, 5 services come from ENGINEERING SERVICE EXAM and medical service come from CENTRAL MEDICAL SERVICE.

CIVIL SERVICE EXAM

From this, following 4 services are recruited:
- INDIAN RAILWAY TRAFFIC SERVICE (IRTS)
- INDIAN RAILWAY PERSONNEL SERVICE (IRPS)
- INDIAN RAILWAY ACCOUNT SERVICE (IRAS)
- INDIAN RAILWAY PROTECTION FORCE (IRPF) –*This name has recently changed.*

ENGINEERING SERVICE EXAM

Following services are recruited through this:
- INDIAN RAILWAY SERVICE OF ENGINEERS (IRSE)
- INDIAN RAILWAY SERVICE OF ELECTRICAL ENGINEER (IRSEE)

- INDIAN RAILWAY SERVICE OF SIGNAL AND TELECOMMUNICATION (IRSST)
- INDIAN RAILWAY STORES SERVICE (IRSS)
- INDIAN RAILWAY SERVICE OF MECHANICAL ENGINEERS (IRSME)

COMBINED MEDICAL SERVICE

Through this, following post is filled:

INDIAN RAILWAY HEALTH SERVICE (IRHS)- Earlier it was called as IRMS (INDIAN RAILWAY MEDICAL SERVICE)

Now, all the above except INDIAN RAILWAY HEALTH SERVICE (IRHS) and INDIAN RAILWAY PROTECTION FORCE SERVICE (IRPFS) have been merged and examinations are conducted as INDIAN RAILWAY MANAGEMENT SERVICE (IRMS).

Earlier, there used to be SCRA (SPECIAL CLASS RAILWAY APPRENTICE) which used to recruit through separate exam SCRA by the UPSC. In this, candidates have to give exam after 12th class and they used to complete mechanical engineering for JAMALPUR and come in the service at an early age. This exam has now been discontinued for two years. This used to be conducted since BRITISH era.

For more information you may visit the website below:

http://www.upsc.gov.in/

Staff is Recruited through:

RAILWAY RECRUITMENT BOARD(RRB)

For recruitment of staff specially in technical category, these all recruited through RRB. This is headed by the Chairman and supported by the Secretary.

Through this, following post are filled:
- TICKET COLLECTOR
- JUNIOR ENGINEER in all department
- TECHNICIAN in all department
- COMMERCIAL CLERK
- MINISTERIAL STAFF
- GUARD AND LOCO PILOT (RAILWAY DRIVER)

These all recruitment are done on COMPUTER BASED TEST(CBT). Hence total transparency & efficiency is maintained.

For more information you may visit the website below:

http://www.rrbmumbai.gov.in/

RAILWAY RECRUITMENT CELL(RRC)

These are specially formed to do recruitment of non-technical staff

at zonal level. Through this, following staff are recruited:
- KHALASI
- PEON
- TRACKMEN
- HELPER, etc

Salary:
Seventh pay commission is applicable to all staff and officers and get as per their rank. Additional Benefits - Medical Facilities, Transportation Facilities, Railway Pass Facilities etc.

SOCIAL MEDIA CAREER

In recent time, Industrialist RATAN TATA said in an interview that our 40% youth will earn money through social media. This is the power of social media.

From this statement, we can understand what the present situation is and what would be the direction of youth in the future. Now with COVID 19, again all countries' equations will change the world in the coming time. Due to this, digitalization will grow fast, and India's Image will become more positive in the future. Also, more and more economy will become digitized, and more tax will come from the service sector. No doubt the agriculture and medical sector will get more boost.

In this perspective, following are the areas where you can earn money in social media:
- BLOG WRITING
- WEBSITE LAUNCH
- TWITTER (Now 'X')
- YOUTUBE VIDEOS
- YOUTUBE CHANNEL
- INSTAGRAM
- DIGITAL MARKETING
- E-MAIL MARKETING
- E-BOOK LAUNCHING

Through this, you can earn money which no one can imagine. In each, earning potential is different and it depends on your expertise, potential and your hard work in it.

Following are the things which required for making your material content rich:
- You should have excellent content which you post in the blog, launching a book on a website or on social media.
- You must have expertise in which you are making comments and writing any blog on the subject.
- You should have the best content which you are publishing on social media.
- Always put the best material. No need to publish videos continuously. You may launch 2-3 videos on social media but need to be worthy.

Salary:
The Average Salary of Social Media Administrator/ Specialist/ Account Manager varies between Rs 3-7 lakh/annum. One can earn more with more experienced and hard work.

What Should You Do?
First you should understand how it works. Learn about it from google, or any other search engine. You can learn through 217 YOUTUBE videos. Many good videos are available and learn through it easily. You can search on YOUTUBE, GOOGLE by querying:
- How to launch an e-book?
- How to earn through blogs?

You will get multiple options and you can choose.

Secondly develop your expertise in this field through your study, education and hard work. For this, you must associate and collaborate with expert people. By this way, you will get to learn in a short period with their experience.

Thirdly you must have knowledge about the IT field and have a tendency & attitude to learn. You must learn AFFILIATE MARKETING, DIGITAL MARKETING, EMAIL MARKETING etc.

Always choose ideas continuously with due care and work hard on those ideas.

Investment: I would say it is zero rupee, but you can take in a single digit thousand-rupee figure. Only your computer and your expert knowledge.

Earning: In thousands to lakh rupees provided you have knowledge and proper implementation.

Future Prospectus: From above words, you could understand what future prospects of social media & Employment would be. Tomorrow education will come on digital mode and social media will increase multifold.

FLY HIGH IN GOVERNMENT FIRM

Various services are available where people can enter after qualifying in the examination. Anyone who did graduation or PG, they can apply for the central and state civil service exam.

- After Graduation
- After post-graduation
- Social Services - Own NGO / Work for NGO.
- Political Career- Symbiosis Political Leadership Programme
- After PHD
- Arts / Science / Finance / Management / Economics

TOUGHEST EXAMS IN THE WORLD

Examinations are the living nightmares of every student in the world. As they grow older, the exams keep getting more challenging. Every student feels that they've been facing the most challenging tests to have ever existed. However, deep within, we all know that some exams are more difficult than others.

Exams have been the source of pressure and anxiety for many teenagers globally. Here, we list down the 10 most difficult exams to crack globally. This research is based on student research and overall analysis.

CCIE- Cisco Certified Internetworking Expert

Cisco Networks conducts this examination for the recruitment of Internet experts within their organization. The test is divided into 6 parts within 2 phases. Only the candidates who clear the first phase are certified to appear for the second phase. The practical phase of this exam lasts for 8 hours and has a 1% clearing rate.

GATE- Gratitude Aptitude Test in Engineering

GATE is an all-India level examination which acts as an entrance test for Indian students pursuing engineering. The test opens doors for post graduate courses for the candidates who clear the test. The test is a joint venture between The Indian Institute of Science and the 7 IITs (Indian Institute of Technology) across the country. There is one single paper which consists of both MCQs and numerical questions.

Gaokao

The Gaokao examination is a compulsory exam which is to be given by every high school student in China. The test is mandatory if the student wishes to pursue higher education. Ranked as the 8th most difficult exam to crack globally, it has been the reason for stress and anxiety for many Chinese teenagers.

IIT-JEE – Indian Institute of Technology Joint Entrance Examination

The Indian Institute of Technology Joint Entrance Examination is an exam which is to be cleared by Indian engineering aspirants who wish to enter one of the 7 most prestigious engineering institutes in India. The exam is divided into 2 objective papers of three hours each. It is totally objective and has a low clearing rate. Out of the 500000 candidates who appear for the exam every year, just 10000 get selected.

UPSC- Union Public Service Commission
This central agency in India conducts all major examinations and to recruit all the top-notch government officials in the country. It is considered as the most difficult Indian Examination. Even the people who clear IIT and GATE find it difficult to clear this exam. Out of nearly 300,000 candidates appearing annually, merely 1,000 of them are selected.

Mensa
The Mensa Society is a global society consisting of people with the highest IQs. Every country has its own Mensa Society, and it's the oldest and the largest IQ organization in the world. The Mensa IQ Test is the most difficult IQ Test in the world and only the cream of the applicant's population is accepted into the society. The lowest IQ present in the society too is the mind-boggling 98 percentile. There is no age bar and its youngest member is 2 years old.

GRE- Graduate Record Examinations
GRE is one of the most widely taken tests globally and also one of the most difficult to crack. Most of every US Universities providing higher education requires all of its applicants to have a specified GRE Score. It is available in online as well as offline modes.

CFA- Chartered Financial Analyst
The CFA is not exactly an examination degree. It is more of a professional stature. The Wall Street Journal has ranked it as the most difficult exam in the world. Less than 1/5th of the applicants clears each year, that too after repeated attempts. The test consists of two objective and one essay type subjective phase.

All Souls Prize Fellowship Exam
This fellowship exam conducted by Oxford University's All Souls College is considered as the second most challenging exam in the world. Until quite recently, the applicants were supposed to write a 222 single essay based on just one word in the paper. It requires a tremendous amount of factual knowledge and a highly imaginative mind. Only two candidates are selected for fellowship every year.

UPSC-CIVIL SERVICE EXAMINATION

Civil Service Examination is one of the toughest examinations in the World. This is an exam through which all premier services posts are filled. Hence this is the most sought exam for which lakhs of candidates apply. It requires rigorous preparation to crack it. Through this, you can become IAS, IFS, IPS, IRS, IRPS etc. Once you are through, you are in the premier post of Indian Government.

Following are the post:

- Armed Forces Headquarters Civil Service, Group 'B' (Section Officer's Grade).
- Delhi, Andaman & Nicobar Islands, Lakshadweep, Daman & Diu and Dadra & Nagar Haveli Civil Service, Group 'B'.
- Delhi, Andaman & Nicobar Islands, Lakshadweep, Daman & Diu and Dadra & Nagar Haveli Police Service, Group 'B'
- Indian Administrative Service
- Indian Civil Accounts Service, Group 'A'
- Indian Corporate Law Service, Group "A"
- Indian Defence Accounts Service, Group 'A'
- Indian Defence Estates Service, Group 'A'
- Indian Foreign Service
- Indian Information Service (Junior Grade), Group 'A'
- Indian Ordnance Factories Service, Group 'A' (Assistant Works Manager, Administration)
- Indian P & T Accounts & Finance Service, Group 'A'.
- Indian Police Service
- Indian Postal Service, Group 'A'
- Indian Audit and Accounts Service, Group 'A'
- Indian Railway Management Service, Group 'A'
- Indian Revenue Service (Customs & Central Excise), Group 'A'
- Indian Revenue Service (I.T.), Group 'A'
- Indian Trade Service, Group 'A'
- Pondicherry Civil Service, Group 'B'
- Pondicherry Police Service, Group 'B'
- Post of Assistant Security Commissioner in Railway Protection Force, Group 'A'

Plan of Examination:

The Civil Services Examination will consist of two successive stages (vide Appendix I Section-I) Each candidate has to fill the preference for the service before facing the interview before the UPSC panel.

List of Optional Subjects for Main Examination:

Following are the optional subjects which can be chosen by the candidate while giving the main examination.

Agriculture	Management
Animal Husbandry and Veterinary Science	Mathematics
Anthropology	Mechanical Engineering
Botany	Medical Science
Chemistry	Philosophy
Civil Engineering	Physics
Commerce and Accountancy	Political Science and International Relations
Economics	Psychology / Public Administration /Sociology
Electrical Engineering/ Geography / Geology / History	Statistics
Law	Zoology

Literature of Any one of the following Languages & Syllabus:

Assamese, Bengali, Bodo, Dogri, Gujarati, Hindi, Kannada, Kashmiri, Konkani, Maithili, Malayalam, Manipuri, Marathi, Nepali, Odia, Punjabi, Sanskrit, Santhali, Sindhi, Tamil, Telugu, Urdu and English.

Syllabus:

Part A—Preliminary Examination

Paper I - (200 marks)

Duration: Two hours

- Current events of national and international importance. History of India and Indian National Movement.
- Indian and World Geography-Physical, Social, Economic Geography of India and the World.
- Indian Polity and Governance-Constitution, Political System, Panchayati Raj, Public Policy, Rights Issues, etc.

Paper II - (200 marks)

Duration: Two hours

- Comprehension
- Interpersonal skills including communication skills
- Logical reasoning & analytical ability

- Decision making & problem solving
- General mental ability
- Basic numeracy (numbers & their relations, orders of magnitude, etc) (Class X level), Data interpretation (charts, graphs, tables, data sufficiency etc. - Class X level)

Civil Service Mains Examination Format:

Paper	Subject	Marks
Paper A	(One of the Indian languages listed below, to be selected by the candidate from the languages listed in the Eighth Schedule to the Constitution of India) (Qualifying)	300
Paper B	English (Qualifying)	300
Paper I	Essay	250
Paper II	General Studies I (Indian heritage and culture, history and geography of the world and society)	250
Paper III	General Studies II (Governance, constitution, polity, social justice and international relations)	250
Paper IV	General Studies III (Technology, economic development, bio-diversity, environment, security and disaster management)	250
Paper V	General Studies IV (ethics, integrity and aptitude)	250
Papers VI, VII	Two papers on one subject to be selected by the candidate from the list of optional subjects below (250 marks for each paper)	500
Sub Total (Written Test)		1750
Personality Test (Interview)		275
Total Marks		2025

Civil Service Interview:

It is also called the "Personality Test". The objective of the interview is to assess the personal suitability of the candidate for a career in public service by a board of competent and unbiased observers. The test is intended to evaluate the mental calibre of a candidate. In broad terms, this is really an assessment of not only a candidate's intellectual qualities, but also social traits and interest in current affairs. Some of the qualities to be judged are mental alertness, critical powers of assimilation, clear and logical exposition, balance of judgement, variety and depth of interest, ability for social cohesion and leadership, and intellectual and moral integrity.

IAS PREPARATION FOR BEGINNERS

While the decision to appear for the UPSC Civil Services Exam may be easy, what follows afterwards is an overwhelming as well as humbling experience. For a beginner the initial months are spent just in understanding what this exam is about and figuring the right path to follow to reach their goal. I can say this with confidence because this is not just my story but every aspirant's. When it comes to the IAS Exams, the MEANS you adopt will ultimately decide whether you reach the END!

Here I share a few tips that will guide you through the labyrinth of UPSC preparation.

Read the Syllabus Carefully:
One of the main reasons that students wander far and deep while studying for UPSC is that they do not pay heed to the syllabus. You neither need too vast knowledge nor too profound. The UPSC needs people who know something about everything and not specialists. If you stick to the syllabus and understand exactly what they want, you will be able to limit your preparation to things that matter.
Also, each subject has dynamic elements, some more than others, so being clear about the syllabus will also help you pick out the right news and put a cap on your current affairs preparation as well. Eventually your own current affairs can be very extensive, but once you integrate it with the syllabus and the previous year's questions, you will not have any trouble in selecting the news you need to read.

Once you know the syllabus, then you can take the right path and avoid unnecessary study material.

Practice Being the Planner, they want:
As an IAS officer, planning should be your forte. Put that skill to test right away by designing a strategy to follow for the remaining one year. Do not rely on coaching institutes for this task, remember, you know yourself best. Plan your studies in a way that helps you optimize your output.

This should be easy once you understand the syllabus and structure of the exam. You can take inspiration from other toppers but alter their strategy to your personality.

Zero Down on Sources:
There are tons of books and heaps of reading material for this coveted exam. As a result, finding the source that is most reliable, authentic and comprehensive becomes quite a task. My suggestion here would be to do a cursory reading of the books suggested by others and then pick the ones you feel are best suited.

Do not buy books online until you have physically gone through them and feel they will be helpful in your prep. No matter which supplementary books you refer to, there is no alternative to NCERTs. Always start your prep from them and then move on.

Save the Notes for Last:
Do not begin making notes the moment you start a certain subject. Consult at least 1-2 sources besides the NCERT, highlight the important points as you read and then compile them into notes.

Devote the maximum time to making notes as this is what you will be referring to in the last few months of your prep. You will not have the time to go through all the books at this stage, therefore put everything that is important in your notes.

Make Revision A Habit:
As you read more, you tend to forget the old. Therefore, make it a point to first revise the previous days notes before gathering new information on a topic. Revising everyday will take you less time than finishing an entire topic and then reading it again. For example, I made notes from PIB and Hindu everyday as part of my current affairs.

The next day, before writing the new information, I would

revise yesterday's notes as well as give a cursory reading to all the notes done before. This helped me retain more information.

A Strong Foundation Is the Key:
When you begin your prep, there will be lots of times when you would wish that you had paid more attention in school. For those who did, the preparation becomes easier because they just have to build further on it and not start from scratch.

There were a lot of topics I encountered for which I just had to study the advanced bits. But don't lose heart if your concepts are not clear.

There is ample time to read the NCERTs and understand them. At this age, your level of comprehension has increased, and you will easily grasp the concepts from the junior class NCERTs. Do not attempt to study the advanced topics before you clear your basics. This approach will only dishearten you and make the easy topic appear difficult.

Reading the Newspaper Is the First Step:
Subscribe to The Hindu/Indian Express as well as get the PIB app, the day you decide to appear for this exam.

You may reserve different days for different subjects, but the newspaper is and should be a daily staple till the interview stage. Reading the news and staying up to date with current affairs is not only crucial as per the new trend of questions, it also helps in shaping your personality.

Being well-read and having knowledge on a certain matter gives you an inherent confidence that reflects in your demeanour. Don't just read the news, find the background, analyse it and then critique it too. This habit will also help you write better answers in the Mains, regardless of the subject as well as perform well in the interview.

Reduce your online as well as offline socializing:
The Civil Services exam is not called the mother of all exams for no reason! Preparing for it requires not just hard work and perseverance, but also altering your lifestyle. An important change to make would be to limit the use of social media as well as your social interactions with the world.

You will have to get your priorities straight for the one year of your prelim's preparation and the six months of Mains exam afterwards.

Set Deadlines:
Setting personal goals for the day as well as months is an excellent way to finish the syllabus in time and get the maximum out of your day. I found it extremely useful and beneficial in preparation. By setting deadlines and a time limit for everything, I was able to optimize my time. It helped me focus on my studies and flush out other redundant activities. Design a timetable for yourself and you will see the difference in both the quantity as well as quality of your studies.

Keep the Fire Burning:
The preparation for UPSC tends to tire you and there will be times when you feel like giving up. But rather than giving up all need to try to find ways to keep going.

One thing that really helped all to listen to the topper's interviews. Hearing about their journey, identifying with their challenges and realizing that they are as human as me, was a satisfying experience. It kept you all on track and infused new motivation.

Online Video Lectures:
To understand the concept, you can watch online videos for a lot of topics. Not only do they help you grasp a topic better, but they also save your time. For example, if reading and comprehending a topic took you an hour on your own, you can do the same by just watching a 15-minute video.

INDIAN ENGINEERING SERVICES EXAM

Under this, following are the services which are recruited through this examination. Later, they work under various ministries like Railway, Defence, Public Work department, Ministry of Road Transport, Ministry of Telecommunication, Border Road Organisation, etc.

- I.R.S.E.
- I.R.S.M.E.
- I.R.S.E.E.
- I.R.S.S.E.
- I.R.S.S.
- C.E.S. Group 'A'
- CE&MES Gr 'A'
- Directorate General Ordnance Factories I.O.F.S. Group 'A'
- Ministry of Road Transport and Highways Central Engineering Service (Roads) Gr. 'A'
- Ministry Of Telecommunication and Information Technology, Department. of Telecommunication
- Indian Telecommunication Service Group 'A', J.T.O (G.C.S. Gr. 'B')
- Ministry of Defence, Department. of Defence Production,
- Directorate General of Aeronautical Quality Assurance
- Defence Aeronautical Quality Assurance Service (DAQAS) Gr 'A'
- Ministry of Science and Technology, Department. of Science and Technology Survey of India Gr 'A' Service
- Geological Survey of India Assistant Executive Engineer Gr 'A'
- Border Roads Organization BRES Gr. 'A'
- Indian Navy Indian Naval Armament Service, Assistant. Naval Store Officer Grade-I
- Military Engineer Services Indian Defence Service of Engineers (IDSE) Group 'A' AEE(QS&C) in Military Engineer Service (MES) Survey

INDIAN FOREST SERVICES EXAM

This is an All-India Service among 3 services which is recruited through separate examination. This is one of the sought posts after IAS, IPS post.

Plan of the Examination:

The competitive examination comprises two successive stages:

- Civil Services (Preliminary) Examination (Objective Type) for the screening & selection of candidates for Indian Forest Service (Main) Examination
- Indian Forest Service (Main) Examination (Written and Interview) for the selection of candidates against the vacancies identified and reported for the Indian Forest Service Examination.

The preliminary Examination will consist of two papers of Objective type (multiple choice questions) and carry a maximum of 400 marks in the subjects set out in sub-section of Section II. This examination is meant to serve as a screening test only; the marks obtained in the Preliminary Examination by the candidates who are declared qualified for admission to the Main Examination will not be counted for determining their final order of merit.

Only those candidates who are declared by the Commission to have qualified in the Preliminary Examination in the year will be eligible for admission to the Main Examination of that year provided they are otherwise eligible for admission to the Main Examination.

Note I : Since there may be common candidates for Civil Services Examination and the Indian Forest Service Examination, after the common Screening Test done through Civil Services (Preliminary) Examination, separate lists will be prepared for the candidates eligible to appear in the Civil Service (Main) Examination and Indian Forest Service (Main) Examination, based on the criterion of minimum qualifying marks of 33% in General Studies Paper-II of Civil Services (Preliminary) Examination and total qualifying marks of General Studies Paper-I of Civil Services (Preliminary) Examination as determined by the Commission on the number of vacancies to be filled through the Civil Services Examination and Indian Forest Service Examination.

Note II: There will be negative marking for incorrect answers. The written examination consisting of the following papers:
- Paper I—General English 300 Marks
- Paper II—General Knowledge 300 Marks
- Papers III, IV, V and VI. —Any two subjects to be selected from the list of the optional subjects set out in para 2 below.

Each subject will have two papers. — 200 marks for each paper. Note: Answer scripts of only those candidates who have obtained the minimum marks as decided by the Commission for Paper II (General Knowledge) will be evaluated.

Interview for Personality Test of such candidates as may be called by the Commission— Maximum Marks: 300

List of optional subjects:
- Agriculture
- Agricultural Engineering
- Animal Husbandry & Veterinary Science
- Botany
- Chemistry
- Chemical Engineering
- Civil Engineering
- Forestry
- Geology
- Mathematics
- Mechanical Engineering
- Physics
- Statistics
- Zoology Provided that the candidates will not be allowed to offer the following combination of subjects:
    - Agriculture and Agricultural Engg.
    - Agriculture and Animal Husbandry & Veterinary Science
    - Agriculture and Forestry
    - Chemistry and Chemical Engg.
    - Mathematics and Statistics
    - Of the Engineering subjects viz. Agricultural Engineering, Chemical Engineering, Civil Engineering and Mechanical Engineering—not more than one subject.

CENTRAL ARMED POLICE FORCES

Through this examination, a candidate can start their career as an Assistant Commandant in following paramilitary forces.

- CENTRAL RESERVE POLICE FORCE- CRPF
- BORDER SECURITY FORCES - BSF
- CENTRAL INDUSTRIAL SECURITY FORCES - CISF
- INDO TIBETAN BORDER POLICE - ITBP
- SASHATRA SEEMA BAL - SSB

Selection Procedure / Scheme & Syllabus of the Exam:

Written Examination: Conduct by UPSC and have 2 papers.

Paper I: General Ability and Intelligence - 250 Marks (The questions in this paper will be of Objective.)

Paper II: General Studies, Essay and Comprehension - 200 Marks In this paper candidates will be allowed the option of writing the Essay Component in English or Hindi, but the medium of Precise Writing, Comprehension Components and other communications/ language skills will 8 be English only. Paper-I will be evaluated first and evaluation of Paper-II will be done only for those candidates who obtain the minimum qualifying marks in Paper-I.

Physical Standards/Physical Efficiency Tests and Medical Standards Tests: Candidates who are declared qualified in the written examination will be summoned for Physical Standards/ Physical Efficiency Tests and Medical Standards Tests. Those candidates who meet the prescribed Physical Standards, specified in Appendix-VI, will be put through the Physical Efficiency Tests as indicated below: Physical Efficiency Tests (PET)

Males & Females

- 100 Meters race in 16 seconds in 18 seconds
- 800 Meters race in 3 minutes 45 seconds in 4 minutes 45 seconds
- Long Jump 3.5 Meters 3.0 meters (3 chances) (3 chances)
- Shot Put (7.26 Kgs.) 4.5 Meters — Pregnancy at the time of PET will be a disqualification and pregnant female candidates will be rejected.

Syllabus of the Written Papers:

Paper I: General Ability and Intelligence The objective type questions with multiple choices in this paper will broadly cover the following areas:

- General Mental Ability
- General
- Current Events of National and International Importance
- Indian Polity and Economy
- History of India

Paper II: General Studies, Essay and Comprehension

Part-A – Essay questions which are to be answered in long narrative form either in Hindi or English totalling 80 Marks. The indicative topics are modern Indian history especially of the freedom struggle, geography, polity and economy, knowledge of security and human rights issues, and analytical ability.

Part-B – Comprehension, precise writing, other communications/ language skills – to be attempted in English only (Marks 120)

The topics are Comprehension passages, precise writing, developing counter arguments, simple grammar and other aspects of language testing.

For more information you may visit the website below:
https://www.drishtiias.com/daily-updates/daily-news-analysis/central-armed-police-force-capf

NATIONAL DEFENCE ACADEMY & NAVAL ACADEMY

Education Qualification:

For Army Wing of National Defence Academy:

12th Class pass of the 10+2 pattern of School Education or equivalent examination conducted by a State Education Board or a University.

For Air Force and Naval Wings of National Defence Academy and for the 10+2 Cadet Entry Scheme at the Indian Naval Academy:

12th Class pass of the 10+2 pattern of School Education or equivalent with Physics and Mathematics conducted by a State Education Board.

Candidates who are appearing in the 12th Class under the 10+2 pattern of School Education or equivalent examination can also apply for this examination.

Scheme of Examination:

Paper-1 Mathematics - 300 Marks
Paper-2 General Ability Test - 600 Marks
SSB Interview – 900

The papers in all the subjects will consist of objective type questions only

Syllabus of Examination:

Paper-1 Mathematics – 300 Marks

ALGEBRA, MATRICES AND DETERMINANTS, TRIGONOMETRY, ANALYTICAL GEOMETRY OF TWO AND THREE DIMENSIONS, DIFFERENTIAL CALCULUS, INTEGRAL CALCULUS AND DIFFERENTIAL EQUATIONS, VECTOR ALGEBRA, STATISTICS AND PROBABILITY.

Paper-2 General Ability Test - 600 Marks

Part 'A'—ENGLISH (Maximum Marks—200)

The syllabus covers various aspects like: Grammar and usage, vocabulary, comprehension and cohesion in extended text to test the candidate's proficiency in English.

Part 'B'—GENERAL KNOWLEDGE (Maximum Marks— 400)

- Section 'A' (Physics)
- Section 'B' (Chemistry)
- Section 'C' (General Science)

- Section 'D' (History, Freedom Movement etc)
- Section 'E' (Geography)
- Section 'F' (Current Events)

Intelligence & Personality Test:

SSB Interview – 900 Marks

The SSB procedure consists of two stage Selection processes – Stage I and Stage II.

Only those candidates who clear the stage I are permitted to appear for stage II.

The details are:

Stage I comprises of Officer Intelligence Rating (OIR) tests are Picture Perception * Description Test (PP&DT). The candidates will be shortlisted based on combination of performance in OIR Test and PP&DT.

Stage II comprises of Interview, Group Testing Officer Tasks, Psychology Tests and the Conference. These tests are conducted over 4 days. The details of these tests are given on the website joinindianarmy.nic.in. The personality of a candidate is assessed by three different assessors viz. The Interviewing Officer (IO), Group Testing Officer (GTO) and the Psychologist.

STATE PUBLIC SERVICE EXAMINATION

It is the best exam at the level of state. It is conducted every year by MPSC to recruit officers into the different areas of the state departments under Maharashtra State Government and conducted by the Maharashtra Public Service Commission (MPSC).

Syllabus:

Examination is conducted in three stages: Prelims, Mains and Interview. Candidates must clear each stage in order to be eligible for the next stage.

Prelim Exam Pattern:

Paper-1 - Objective - 100 Questions - 200 Marks - 2 Hours
Paper-2 - Objective - 80 Questions - 200 Marks - 2 Hours

Please keep following things in mind:

No doubt it is an exam of knowledge but it is also a skill. Many students even having knowledge, they could not crack prelims due 245 committing many mistakes in the exam hall. They do wrong questions and get more negative marks and get failed. Hence, they should do more objective questions practice. Marks of both papers will be considered for qualifying candidates for the mains exam.

There will be no negative marking if you do not answer questions. There is negative marking and 1/3 of the marks allocated to the question for wrong questions. This is screening in nature.

Need to score minimum marks as decided to qualify for the mains exam. All the questions are set in English and Marathi.

MPSC Mains Exam Pattern: Once you qualify the Prelims, you are eligible to appear for the Mains Exam. There are no optional subjects in the Mains exam.

Paper-1 - Marathi & English (Essay/Translation/Precise)- 100 Marks
Paper-2 - Marathi & English (Grammar/Comprehension)- 100 Marks
Paper-3 - General Studies 1 - 150 Marks
Paper-4 - General Studies 2 - 150 Marks
Paper-5 - General Studies 3 - 150 Marks
Paper-6 - General Studies 4 - 150 Marks

MPSC Interview: This is typically based on your general knowledge and communication skill. Your ability to tackle a situation and genuineness for a job is rectified. Ultimately your nature with knowledge makes you able to handle the public.

State Public Service Commission:
Following are the posts filled

- ASSISTANT DIRECTOR, STATE FINANCE AND ACCOUNT SERVICE
- ASSISTANT PROJECT OFFICER - TECH-GR B
- ASSISTANT REGIONAL TRANSPORT OFFICER- GR B
- ASSISTANT SALES TAX COMMISSIONER
- BLOCK DEVELOPMENT OFFICER-GR B
- CHIEF OFFICER OF MUNICIPAL COUNCIL
- DEPUTY DIRECTOR. INDUSTRY-TECHNICAL
- DY COLLECTOR
- DY DIRECTOR, STATE EDUCATION SERVICE
- DY SP
- NAIB TAHSILDAR- GR B
- SALES TAX OFFICER
- SECTION OFFICER- GR B
- STATE ENGINEERING SERVICE
- STATE FOREST SERVICE
- STATE GR EXAMINATION
- TAHSILDAR-EXECUTIVE MAGISTRATE

Exam pattern and syllabus is the same as UPSC with some changes vary state to state.

For more information you may visit the website below:
https://www.indiaeducation.net/civil_services/upsc/csexam/exam-patter

FOREIGN EDUCATION

After 12th - DIRECT ADMISSION FOR BACHELOR'S DEGREE, this is possible when child is taking education in the international institution like CAMBRIDGE school or OXFORD school who latter get admission into the UK Universities based on the score take by them in the school without following methodology of GRE AND TOFEL.

Whereas after graduation, students in INDIA give GRE and TOFEL, get universities abroad based on their score and get scholarships accordingly. Based on background and GRE, GATE, GMAT SCORE, they get admission in MS in various categories like engineering, physics, biomedical, maths, other or MBA in finance, HR, operation,

PhD- Normally IN USA AND EUROPE, it requires 5 years to complete a doctorate where there is an inbuilt master's degree they give. It is very rigorous, intensive coursework where students have to give their 100%. Once they complete, they really achieve extensive in their area of work.

To get financial support from various trusts and institutions, following scholarships are available for those who have a nice GRE score.

If you have talent and you are ready to do hard work, then it is not difficult to get admission in foreign universities. Once you get a nice GRE score, your 90% problem is over. Education to get masters or doctoral degrees from top 100 universities of the reputed institutions. Once you do, you will be a noteworthy person and you get a lot of opportunities at national as well as international level. But it is not difficult to get it. If you get the best GRE score and you see what scholarships are available for you with great care, then it would not be difficult for you to get admission without any expenditure provided you should have an excellent GRE score and right guidance for application to university.

For Study in Asia:

- Aichi Scholarship Program for Asian Students in Japan
- DST A*STAR Call for Singapore-India Joint Research Grants
- Hinrich Full MA Scholarship in International Journalism at HKBU

- HM King's and HM Queen's Scholarships for Asian Students in Thailand
- Silk-Road Scholarship Program at Seoul National University

For Study in Australia:
- University of Adelaide Ashok Khurana Scholarship for Indian Students
- India Global Leaders Scholarship
- University of New South Wales (UNSW Sydney) Future of Change India Scholarship

For Study in Europe:
- UCD Global Graduate Scholarships for Indian Students in Ireland
- Orange Tulip Scholarship (The Netherlands)
- Campus France Charpak Scholarship (France)
- Agatha Harrison Memorial Fellowship (United Kingdom)
- British Council GREAT scholarships for Indian Students (UK)
- Charles Wallace India Trust Scholarships (UK)
- Oxford and Cambridge Society of India (OCSI) Scholarships (UK)
- Saltire Scholarships (UK)
- Sir Ratan Tata Fellowships for South Asian Students at LSE (UK
- Sussex India Scholarships (UK)
- University of Bournemouth Business School Dean's Scholarships for Masters Students (UK)
- University of Lincoln India Scholarship (UK)
- UWE International Scholarships (UK)

For Study in USA:
- Asian Women in Business Scholarship Fund
- Chicago Booth School of Business
- Cornell University Tata Scholarship
- Fulbright-Nehru Research Fellowships
- S.N. Bose Scholars Student Exchange Program for Indian Students
- Stanford Reliance Dhirubhai Fellowships for Indian students

NATIONAL OVERSEAS SCHOLARSHIP SCHEME

Objective of the Scheme: The Central Sector Scheme of National Overseas Scholarship is to facilitate the low-income students belonging to the Scheduled Castes, Denotified Nomadic and Semi-Nomadic Tribes, Landless Agricultural Labourers and Traditional Artisans category to obtain higher education in following programme- Master degree or Ph.D. courses by studying abroad thereby improving their Economic and Social status.

Scope:
- In each Selection Year, 100 fresh awards, subject to availability of funds, will be given under the Scheme.

The Scheme provides financial assistance to the selected candidates for pursuing Masters level courses and Ph.D. courses abroad in the Institutions/Universities accredited by the Government/ an authorized body of that country in any fields of study.

- The following is the category wise distribution Category Numbers
    - Scheduled Castes: 90
    - Denotified, Nomadic and Semi-Nomadic Tribes: 06
    - Landless Agricultural Labourers & Traditional Artisans: 04
    - **Total Slots: 100**
    - 30% of the awards for each year shall be earmarked for women candidates.

Who are not eligible under this programme?
- Bachelors Level courses in any discipline are not covered under the Scheme.
- Candidates already staying/ studying abroad are not eligible for scholarship under the Scheme.

Candidates having unconditional offer of admission to top 1000 ranked foreign Institutes/Universities as per the latest available QS ranking only will be selected for grant of scholarship during the first three rounds of selection out of a total of four rounds in the selection year.

During the fourth cycle of selection priority will be given as follows:
- Candidates having unconditional offer letter of admission from Top 1000 QS Ranking Institutions applying in the fourth cycle.
- Candidates having unconditional offer letter of admission from other recognized Institutions who have applied for scholarship under the scheme during the previous cycles or current cycle.
- Candidates submitting proof of applying in any recognized institution applying for scholarship under the scheme in any of the cycles.

However, any financial condition mentioned in the offer of admission such as deposit of fee or any other amount, or proof of source of funds, shall not be a bar for consideration of application under the Scheme guidelines.

Minimum Qualification:
In order to be eligible for scholarship, at least 60% of marks or equivalent grade in the qualifying examination would be required.

In case of Ph. D courses, the qualifying exam would be Master's Degree and for Master's Degree courses, the qualifying examination would be Bachelor's Degree.

Age:
Not more than 35 (Thirty-Five) years, as on the first day of April, 2020.

Income Ceiling:
Total family income from all sources shall not exceed Rs. 8.00 lakh per annum in the preceding year, i.e., 2019-20.

Maximum Number:
Maximum Number of children in a family for the award Not more than two children of the same parents/guardians will be eligible for scholarship under the scheme and a self-certification will be required from the candidate to this effect.

www.nosmsje.gov.in : The portal shall be opened for calling of applications from April of every year for a period of 30 days and only online applications received shall be considered for award in the first cycle of selection. In case the slots remain unfilled, the portal will be again opened every quarter for a period of 30 days (i.e. from 1st July to 30th July, of every year, 1st October, to 30th October, and 1st January, next year to 30th January, until all the slots are filled. Once all the 100 slots are filled, the portal will not be reopened for submission of applications.

Selection Procedure:

Initially, only candidates who have obtained unconditional offers of admission from one of the foreign Institutions/ Universities which are in the list of top 1000 ranked institutions/ universities from the academic session of a particular year. The online applications of the eligible candidates shall be placed before the Selection-cum-Screening Committee for making their recommendations for selection and ranking. Maharashtra Government Scholarship for Foreign Education is available for those candidates who have secured admission in top 100 universities as per QS OR TIMES ranking. All should fulfil demands as per conditions given by the government department.

This information is available in detail on following website:
http://dtemaharashtra.gov.in/foreignscholarship2019/index.html

GRADUATE RECORD EXAMINATION (GRE)

The Graduate Record Examinations (GRE) is a standardized test that is an admissions requirement for many graduate schools in the United States and Canada. The GRE is owned and administered by Educational Testing Service (ETS).

According to ETS, the GRE aims to measure verbal reasoning, Financial Math, analytical writing, and critical thinking skills that have been acquired over a long period of learning. The GRE consists of certain specific algebra, geometry, arithmetic, and vocabulary sections.

The importance of a GRE score can range from being a mere admission formality to an important selection factor. The GRE was significantly overhauled in August 2011, resulting in an exam that is not adaptive on a question-by-question basis, but rather by section, so that the performance on the first verbal and math sections determines the difficulty of the second sections presented.

Overall, the test retained the sections and many of the question types from its predecessor, but the scoring scale was changed to a 130 to 170 scale (from a 200 to 800 scale). The cost to take the test is US$205.

SCHOLASTIC ASSESSMENT TEST (SAT)

The Scholastic Assessment Test (SAT) is a standardized test, owned and published by the College Board, and widely used for college admissions in the United States. Thus, if you intend to apply to a college in the United States, having a good SAT score is crucial for a successful application.

SAT Exam Practice Questions are the simplest way to prepare for the SAT test. Practice is an essential part of preparing for a test and improving at What is the SAT exam used for?

The SAT is a multiple-choice, pencil-and-paper test created and administered by the College Board. The purpose of the SAT is to measure a high school student's readiness for college, and provide colleges with one common data point that can be used to compare all applicants.

Who is eligible for SAT exams?
In the US, typically candidates take the exam in their junior or senior years of high school (Indian Grades 11th or 12th), to be 258 precisely, aspirants are roughly between 17 or 18 years of age when they take the SAT test which is administered by the College Board.

What is the use of the SAT exam in India?
Take the SAT exam in India to study in the US and Canada. Scholastic Assessment Test (SAT) is an entrance exam used by most colleges and universities in the US, Canada as well as other countries to select students for admissions to undergraduate courses.

What SAT score is required for MIT?
For MIT, the average SAT score is between 1500–1570. Nationally, the average composite score is 1000. For Math, MIT accepted students averaged a score of 770–800; nationally the average score was 511. For Reading (sometimes called Verbal) MIT scored an average 750–800.

COMMON ADMISSION TEST (CAT)

The Common Admission Test (CAT) is a computer-based test for admission in a graduate management program. The test scores a candidate on the bases of Quantitative Ability (QA), Verbal Ability (VA) and Reading Comprehension (RC), Data Interpretation (DI) and Logical Reasoning (LR).

What is meant by CAT exam?

CAT (Common Admission Test) is the premier all India management entrance exam conducted by IIMs. Last year 2,04,267 students competed for 1550+ seats making it the most competitive exam in the country. The IIMs are the premier management institutes in India established by an act of Parliament.

Who is eligible for CAT exam?

A candidate is eligible to appear in CAT 2019 if he/she holds a bachelor's degree with at least 50% marks or equivalent CGPA. The candidates belonging to Scheduled Caste (SC), Scheduled Tribe (ST) and Differently Abled (DA) categories, need at least 45% marks.

CAT exam is tough?

The CAT is a yearly exam which increases the stakes by big margin every year. ... Lots of candidates take the CAT exam prep too hard on themselves, and this is not fair. Reason being, CAT is an aptitude exam, and you can do wonders on your day! It isn't a syllabus-based exam.

Is coaching required for CAT?

You need not to opt for coaching. CAT is the exam which tests your reading ability and comprehension, your aptitude for secondary school mathematics and general data sets. If you have good reading skills, vocabulary and you are good at secondary school mathematics then you are almost done with the basic preparation.

POST-DOCTORAL RESEARCH & SCIENTIFIC CAREER

Once you complete Ph.D., Then you can go for post-doctoral studies in various fields like social science or science subjects in India and in foreign universities.

In India, ICSSR sponsor Post-Doctoral Fellowship in various social science subjects as given below:

Main purpose of ICSSR Post-Doctoral Fellowship is to encourage and retain young Indian social science scholars who have completed their PhD and who wish to pursue a regular career in teaching and research which ultimately develop Indian scientific area.

The broad disciplines of study, within the domain of social sciences are:

Commerce
Economics
Environmental Studies
Health Studies
International Studies

Legal Studies
Management
National Security and Strategic Studies
Political Science
Public Administration

Social Anthropology
Social Geography
Social Work
Sociology
Socio-Philosophical Studies

Eligibility
- The scholar should not be more than 45 years at the time of application.

- The scholar must possess a Ph.D. degree in any of the social science disciplines.
- A fellow is required to affiliate himself/herself to an ICSSR Research Institute/ institutes of national importance as approved by MHRD/ government research institutes/ public funded Indian university including deemed university/college having approved Ph.D. programme and requisite research infrastructure of his/her choice.

How to Apply?
- Applications will be invited through advertisements in leading Newspaper(s)/Association of Indian University (AIU) Newsletter and on ICSSR website and should be received before the deadline mentioned in the advertisement. A fellow is required

Duration and Value:
- Post-Doctoral Fellowship is a full-time research work.
- The duration of the fellowship is strictly for two years.
- The value of the fellowship is Rs.31,000 p.m. and contingency grant is Rs.25,000/-p.a.

Conditions:
- Abstract of the Proposal (up to 300 words).
- Detailed Research Proposal (about 3000 words in the format as indicated in the guidelines).
- Brief academic CV (up to three pages including (1) educational qualifications, (post-graduation onwards), (2) list of five best publications in the form of books/research papers/reports with bibliographical details).
- Consent letter and brief academic CV of the Supervisor (2-3 pages).
- Forwarding letter from the Head of the affiliating Institution duly stamped and signed on the letterhead.
- Self-attested Matriculation Certificate and Post-Graduation/M Phil/Ph D. Certificates/Mark sheets.

INTERNATIONAL CAREER - UNITED NATIONS & OTHERS

United Nation is an international body which is working for public service through various branches as given below. Others like the World Bank, World Health Organization etc are its bodies, hence it is called a United Nations Organization. Following are the bodies which are working in their specialized areas at various levels like working in the field for the benefit of the people in different areas.

UN funds and programmes:

Are distinctly different from specialized agencies. In general, the funds and programmes are established by a resolution of the UN General Assembly and have a focused mandate. They are funded either mainly or entirely through voluntary contributions and have a governing body that reviews their activities. The bulk of their funding comes from voluntary contributions from governments, institutions, and individuals. Some specialized agencies, such as the International Labour Organization (ILO), have been in existence longer than the United Nations.

There are currently 17 specialized agencies:

- *Food and Agriculture Organization (FAO)*
- *IBRD: International Bank for Reconstruction and Development*
- *IDA: International Development Association*
- *IFC: International Finance Corporation*
- *International Civil Aviation Organization (ICAO)*
- *International Fund for Agricultural Development (IFAD)*
- *International Labour Organization (ILO)*
- *International Maritime Organization (IMO)*
- *International Monetary Fund (IMF)*
- *International Telecommunications Union (ITU)*
- *United Nations Educational, Scientific and Cultural Organization (UNESCO)*
- *United Nations Industrial Development Organization (UNIDO)*
- *Universal Postal Union (UPU)*
- *World Bank Group*
- *World Health Organization (WHO)*
- *World Intellectual Property Organization (WIPO)*
- *World Meteorological Organization (WMO)*

Top 10 facts about the United Nations:
- The UN was founded after the Second World War to replace the League of Nations which had been so ineffectual in preventing war.
- UN Peacekeeping forces comprise 116,919 field forces from 123 countries.
- The UN provides food to 90 million people.
- The United Nations was awarded the Nobel Peace Prize in 2001.

Headquarters of the United Nations:
Situated In New York City. The logo and flag of the UN have become its symbols as it carries out its work on the world stage. There are six official languages of the UN. These are Arabic, Chinese, English, French, Russian and Spanish.

Membership of the United Nations:
There are currently 193 UN Member States. Each of the Member States of the United Nations has one seat in the General Assembly.

These are strong international agencies which are working through International Civil Servant. These higher officials are recruited through INTERNATIONAL CIVIL SERVICE COMMISSION. These are like the IAS of Indian Government.

This is called the Young Professional Programme in which candidates are recruited in their 20s.

Special written examination and followed by interviews are done. This is a highly lucrative career where this is a combination of INDIAN FOREIGN SERVICE AND INDIAN ADMINISTRATIVE SERVICE seen.

Let us see HOW ICSC carries out examinations and how to apply.

INTERNATIONAL CIVIL SERVICE COMMISSION-ICSC

The International Civil Service Commission (ICSC) is an independent expert body established by the United Nations General Assembly in 1974. Since its inception, the ICSC has redoubled its efforts to strengthen and maintain high standards in the international civil service, while balancing the needs and concerns of its major stakeholders.

This is composed of fifteen members who serve in their personal capacity. Headed by an Executive Secretary, the secretariat is composed of more than 40 staff members.

Professional and Higher Categories:

The Professional and higher categories comprise five Professional grades (P-1 to P-5), two Director levels (D-1 and D-2), as well as the levels of Assistant Secretary-General and 269 Under Secretary-General in some organizations and Assistant Director-General and Deputy Director General in others.

Human Resources Management:

The International Civil Service Commission (ICSC) adopted a framework for human resources management in 2000 to facilitate the effective personnel management and promote common values of international civil service. Many changes have taken place in the world of work in the last decade; therefore, the Commission revised the framework in 2017.

Job Openings in the UN: All job openings in the UNITED NATIONS are available on the following web portal which provides all details: www.careers.un.org

Staff categories: This is important to know what various posts at what levels are. Positions in different staff categories are advertised on the United Nations Careers Portal likewise:

International Recruitment:

Professional and higher categories: Internationally recruited staff performing analytical and conceptual work, normally outside of the country of origin and with the expectation to move geographically throughout their career.

Field Service category: Internationally recruited staff in field operations whose functions range from procedural, operational and technical to analytical and conceptual.

Local Recruitment:

National Professional Officers category: Nationals and permanent residents of the country of service performing analytical and conceptual work within a national context.

General Service category: Staff whose functions range from routine or repetitive to complex and paraprofessional.

Trade and Crafts category: Drivers, electricians, building management staff in New York.

Security Service category: Security officers in New York.

Public Information Assistants category: Tour guides in New York.

Language Teachers category: Language teachers in New York and Geneva.

The movement of staff members from the Field Service category up to the FS-5 level and the General Service and related categories (other than the National Professional Officer category) to the Professional category in the United Nations is exclusively allowed through the Young Professionals Programme competitive examinations. The announcements for these examinations are published on the United Nations Careers Portal.

Job Opening Types:
Job openings are usually advertised to fill specific positions which are available for a period of one year or longer. Some job openings in field operations are only open to rostered candidates who have been preapproved for selection. These job openings are called recruit from roster job openings. To

be preapproved for selection in field operations, applicants may apply for generic job openings which are advertised for that purpose.

Temporary job openings are advertised to fill staff positions available for less than one year. The position may be temporary due to budget constraints or limited duration of need.

Non-Staff Opportunities:
Opportunities for consultant and individual contractor contracts may also be advertised on the United Nations Careers Portal. Consultants are engaged in an advisory or consultative capacity to provide specialized skills or knowledge not normally possessed by staff. Individual contractors may be engaged to perform staff-like work, such as translation, editing or part-time maintenance.

Internship Program:
It is a very good opportunity for young candidates and specially for Indians studying abroad. If you get this chance, you will be able to see it closely and you may apply for the Young Professional Program. Undergraduate students in their final year of studies and graduate students wishing to enhance their educational experience and gain experience in the work of the United Nations may apply for internships on the United Nations Careers Portal. Interns work full-time for two to six months. Interns are not paid.

United Nations Volunteers:
These are individuals who volunteer for at least six months and who are deployed mainly to support field operations. Many of them already have relevant expertise and several years of work experience. United Nations Volunteers receive an allowance. For further information on United Nations Volunteers and on how to apply for these opportunities. visit www.unv.org.

Finding Job Openings:

Best part of it is that any person from the private or government sector can apply for these positions with suitable expertise and experience. All are placed on the same level with equal weightage while putting on a job.

Due to above reasons, who are reading this, either mid-career person or parents or youngsters and have interest to work on international platforms, then this is a great opportunity for them.

The United Nations Careers Portal is the right place to start looking for opportunities in the United Nations. Applicants may also access job openings through Inspira, the United Nations' talent management platform. While both websites may be used to browse and search job openings, applicants must create an account in Inspira to submit applications.

United Nations Careers Portal: https://careers.un.org
Inspira: https://inspira.un.org

- To search job openings in Inspira, applicants need an account. If they already have an account, they may log in to Inspira by entering the username and password.
- Inspira is available in both English and French.
- After logging in, enter keywords such as job title or duty station in the search boxes to look for job openings (1 year or longer) or temporary job openings (less than 1 year). Click *Search*.
- Notifications relating to job applications, job alerts, selections, etc. may be viewed by clicking My Notifications on the Inspira home page.
- To Apply for various positions Applicants must have an account in Inspira

Applying to Job Openings:
During the application process, applicants will be asked to provide details and documentation pertaining to their educational background, work experience, language

proficiency and other qualifications, knowledge and skills. It is important for applicants to elaborate in the application that they satisfy the criteria specified in the job opening. The United Nations may screen applicants through automatic screening, manual review and other evaluation methods.

Once applicants have found a job opening those interests them, they should pay special attention to the criteria specified for education, work experience, languages and competencies.

Applicants are encouraged to apply for job openings for which they at least meet the "required" criteria and have previously demonstrated the specified competencies. Applicants should also pay attention to the competencies stated in the job openings. Applicants may be assessed to determine if they have these competencies through different evaluation and assessment methodologies including a competency-based interview.

After submitting the application, applicants may go through various stages of evaluation and assessment.

Automatic and manual screening:
Upon submission, applications go through an automatic screening process in Inspira based on a set of pre-established rules on age, academic qualifications, length of work experience, family relationships, criminal record and others according to the United Nations Staff Regulations and Rules, applicable policies and requirements of the job opening.

Evaluation:
The hiring managers evaluate the released applicants and create a shortlist of applicants based on the criteria specified in the job opening.

Assessments:
Shortlisted applicants may be invited to participate in assessments such as written exercises, presentations,

technical tests, knowledge-based interviews, competency-based interviews or other assessments. Assessments are normally scheduled for a specific date and time slot. Applicants who do not respond to invitations or cannot be reached by email or phone in a timely manner, or do not participate in assessments will be disqualified.

Competency-based interviews:

For job openings and generic job openings, the competency-based interview is a mandatory assessment methodology. Only a select number of applicants are invited for this interview. The goal of this interview is to gather objective evidence of the applicants' competencies through their past behaviour and performance.

Before the interview, applicants should familiarize themselves with the indicators of each competency stipulated in the job opening and think about the past examples where they demonstrated those indicators.

During the interview, the interview panel normally consisting of three United Nations staff members including the hiring manager, will ask for examples when they have demonstrated the competencies, particularly how they handled or addressed a situation or task.

Applicants may be asked to give both positive and negative examples for some of the competencies. These questions are called behavioural questions. Appraisal and comparison questions may be used to obtain further insight on the applicant's behaviours.

Several probing or follow-up questions may also be asked until the interview panel has gathered sufficient evidence.

The below table shows some examples of different question types which are asked during a competency-based interview:

Behavioural:
Give me an example of...
Please describe a situation when you had to... and how did you go about it?

Appraisal:
What was the feedback you received from your team members?
What feedback did you receive about your role in this project?

Comparison:
In relation to leadership specifically, what makes you stand out as compared to others around you?
Which of your previous experiences working in a team was the best as compared to others, and why?

Probing / Follow-up:
What happened next?
What were your specific responsibilities in the team?
A competency-based interview typically lasts 30 to 60 minutes. Depending on the location of the applicant and availability of communication methodologies, a mix of in-person, video or phone interviews may occur.

Checking application status:
Applicants may check the status of their application in Inspira by clicking My Applications.
Each status has the following meaning:
- Draft means the applicant has started a draft application but has not submitted it.
- Rostered means the applicant was recommended for the job opening although he or she was not selected.
- Selected means the applicant was selected for the job opening.
- Filled from Roster means a rostered applicant was selected.
- JO Cancelled means the job opening was cancelled.

Applicants who are selected for job openings are notified immediately. Selected applicants must confirm their continued interest and availability via email within five business days of the notification. If no confirmation is received within five business days, another applicant may be selected.

Application result: Rostered

All applicants who are recommended for selection and roster placement for job openings and generic job openings, including the selected applicants, are placed on the roster, which is a pool of pre-approved candidates for subsequent job openings at the same level and with similar functions. However, placement on the roster is no guarantee of a future selection or appointment. The scope of the roster may change as determined appropriately by the United Nations Office of Human Resources in the Department of Management Strategy, Policy and Compliance.

Roster candidates receive an invitation to apply when job openings are advertised where they are preapproved for selection. Roster candidates are encouraged to apply as early as possible because the hiring managers may immediately recommend roster candidates for selection without the full evaluation and assessment process

To view roster memberships and details including the level, status, membership start date and associated job titles, click *My Roster Memberships* at the top of the Inspira home page. Candidates may withdraw from the roster or put their roster membership on hold on this page. Once candidates withdraw themselves from a roster, the roster membership cannot be reinstated.

In *My Roster Memberships* page, applicants will also see currently available job openings to which they may apply as roster candidate.

YOUNG PROFESSIONAL PROGRAMME (YPP)

YPP is highly demanded which is not even known in higher class in India. This is an annual initiative focussed on the selection and recruitment of distinguished and highly qualified young professionals from different parts of the World.

Every year, around 50,000 candidates from all pre-selected nations from over the world apply to become International Civil servant with the UNITED NATIONS SECRETARIAT. Once they are selected, they are invited to take part in a professional development programme, afterwards they start their successful career in UNO.

They start their career with a good salary package and good career progression with good career mobility.

Eligibility: Graduate degree minimum
Age: 18-year-old and maximum 32 year
Other:
- From invited nation by UNO
- Knows English or French language
- Should not be relative who is working in UN Secretariat

Study Material:
There is not exact material required in this, but intensive preparation is required. Focus to get material from the site below in respect of specialized paper and general paper including books articles, reports, book publication etc.

Need to do an essay writing paper with giving your presenting skill. Also do practice MCQ. Always to give mock examinations to get mastery in the performance.

Important Information:
This Young Professional Program (YPP) is not only available in the United Nations but also issued by each international agency with their own YPP.
Like WORLD BANK, ASIAN DEVELOPMENT BANK ETC. Every year, they advertise for YPP and conduct examinations for this. Initially they are appointed for fixed term.

According to the requirements of each agency, they notify their required specialization. Ex for WORLD BANK OR ADB, they require specialization in economics and finance. On the other hand, the World Health Organization requires expertise in medicine.

Can reach to learn at following website:
www.openigo.com
http://ypun.org
http://unjobs.org
www.adb.org
www.worldbank.org
http://careers.un.org
www.opprtunitiesforyouth.org

BANK LOAN FOR EDUCATION

This question normally comes up in everybody's life during education or later life. I think, if you have a good score and talent, then money is not a problem. Normally in western countries, children are expected to take loans for higher education. For that purpose, they take out loans and go ahead. During their earning phase, they pay their loan.

Whereas in India, this is considered in different ways which should not be. This is a normal process where children also support their parents by reducing financial burden by taking loans. It is interest free while education goes on and it starts after education is over. Hence it is a good option to get it.

Only problem is that normally banks do not offer loans for normal institutions where they do not have confidence to get it back. If you are taking admission in a top institution which is highly ranked. Then this problem does not come to you. They 284 come to you to give loan to you. It is due to having security to get a loan back with their interest.

Such institutions like below where loan is not problem:

ALL INDIA INSTITUTE OF MEDICAL   *INDIAN INSTITUTE OF TECHNOLOGY*

SCIENCE
INDIAN INSTITUTE OF MANAGEMENT
INDIAN INSTITUTE OF SCIENCE
TOP ENGINEERING COLLEGES
TOP MEDICAL COLLEGES

Banks available for you:

Bank of Baroda
State Bank of India
Punjab National Bank
Union Bank of India

Even though I would like students who have financial need, they must work hard and get good scores and get good, reputed institutions. This will facilitate getting a loan in an easy manner.

FREE EDUCATION WEBSITES

Now the world is changing at a fast pace. Distance does not matter if you have to learn new knowledge. Hence all international universities have opened their education to the outside world for those who could not get admission in their universities and those who have interest to learn new skills.

On this platform following universities provide free online certificate courses:

AUSTRALIAN NATIONAL UNIVERSITY
BERKELEY UNIVERSITY OF CALIFORNIA
BOSTON UNIVERSITY
COLUMBIA UNIVERSITY
GEORGETOWN UNIVERSITY
HARVARD UNIVERSITY
IIT BOMBAY
MASSACHUSETTS INSTITUTE OF TECHNOLOGY
NATIONAL UNIVERSITY OF SINGAPORE
STANFORD UNIVERSITY
TEXAS UNIVERSITY
UNIVERSITY OF BRITISH COLUMBIA
UNIVERSITY OF OXFORD

Many more universities will be found on this online platform. These are below online website who gives information about free courses available in various universities as follows:

www.edx.org & www.coursera.org

These provide 4000 courses in 140 top universities and institution in following subjects:

BUSINESS AND MANAGEMENT
COMPUTER SCIENCE
DATA SCIENCE
ECONOMICS AND FINANCE
ENGINEERING
HUMANITIES
LANGUAGE

There are a huge number of courses in various fields where you can get certificates and master's program degrees.

There are 45 million people taking courses online. From this, we can understand the growth of online courses and its importance and fast exposure to distance education.

Following are the Master's program in following subjects:
- MANAGEMENT- MBA
- INFORMATION TECHNOLOGY
- PUBLIC HEALTH
- ELECTRICAL ENGINEERING
- MACHINE LEARNING

Now, those who are thinking that they do not have money and access to top universities, but from this onward, they should not feel this way and get full benefit.

INTERNATIONAL OPPORTUNITIES

There are great opportunities available in international organizations other than Multinational Companies. These are top institutions where getting work opportunities itself is a great honor. Once you are in, then sky is limit for your growth provided you give full efforts and give full commitment.

You should also focus on the following website where you should take information from where you get knowledge about vacancies and required qualification for that post.

www.worldbank.csod.com

You will get information about vacancies in WORLD BANK and its affiliate organization for Economist, Consultant, Accountant etc.

www.imf.org-job-joboppo or www.imf.org-recruitment

This INTERNATIONAL MONETARY FUND organization where financial policies are made at international level. This also provides loans to various countries when there are financial problems.

www.unjobs.org

You will get all kinds of vacancies in the areas of administration, economist, human resource, and programming. This is the largest international organization among all. Hence opportunities are also huge in number.

From above, you can get to know various opportunities and follow its instructions to fill applications. Once you are in, then growth would depend on your hard work and commitment. Normally on the following site, all UNITED NATION vacancies are available where you can apply through this website. Please study and focus.

www.inspira.un.org

HOW TO CONSISTENTLY BE SUCCESSFUL AND WEALTHY?

Always people say that money is not important. But money is important up to a certain extent. After you get sufficient money, it is not important at all. Then your focus goes on health, family, relatives, friends etc.

Hence, most important thing is to balance between all which are given above.

ADD VALUE TO YOUR KNOWLEDGE

Something many self-made wealthy people have in common is that they are valuable in specific ways. Even when millionaires and billionaires are taken out of the equation, many rich people — doctors, engineers, filmmakers — have gotten rich after adding value to themselves and then adding value to the world. For example, a rich neurosurgeon may be especially talented and skilled. This surgeon added value to the world after improving their own skills and quality of life. Adding value to yourself is a good foundation to begin your journey to being rich. This can be possible with continuous reading and learning processes with the will to improve ourselves.

SAVE YOUR MONEY FIRST, THEN SPEND

The concept of saving money is not a new one. However, it is extremely easy to "dip into your savings" when you want something badly enough. The key to accomplishing your goal of amassing wealth is to try and save money.

A different way of looking at your savings is to view them as taxes. Once you pay your taxes, you never get the whole amount back. Treat your savings the same way. Set money aside in a savings account or transfer it to a totally separate account where you cannot touch it. Treat your savings like money that you will never get back, until the day that you get it all back at once.

CREATE A PLAN AND FOLLOW IT

In this world, nothing comes easily and luckily. Most rich people have made great efforts through their meticulous preparation and hard work. They have created value in it by creating new ideas.

Money cannot be made by thinking only. For this, we need to have ideas, vision to implement, need to plan properly, ability to implement meticulously and quality to chase properly. This all makes a successful plan working. Always success follows with money

START A BUSINESS

If you want to be rich, it is always nice to start your business where you can earn millions of rupees. This is much easier said than done, but the last four steps lay the groundwork to be able to start your own business. If you have a knack for business or want to be your own boss, this can be a great step to making some money. However, as many entrepreneurs will tell you, creating your own business requires massive upfront costs and low revenue in the beginning.

BE GRATEFUL

More you become big; your humbleness goes on increasing. Like the trees with more fruits, branches of trees go down. Hence, it is natural to be grateful, humble etc. Becoming rich does not only require external factors to fall into place — many personality factors have to align for you to succeed at whatever venture you've started. Staying humble and grateful for the progress you've made at every step of the way is essential.

DEVELOP PATIENCE

Nothing can be achieved without patience. Same way, patience is required to earn money which is quite a long process. All the efforts you put towards accumulating wealth could take months or even years to pay off. It's easy to get frustrated early on, especially when it seems like there's a new wealthy person in the news every other day.

EDUCATE YOURSELF

Life is a constant learning process. If you want to grow, you have to educate yourself every day. If you do not educate yourself, you will be out of competition. Successful people average read 60 books per year, even some more than 100 books.

Warren Buffet, investment guru, read for 7-8 hours read every day. From this, you can understand the importance of reading every day.

This means you have to constantly educate yourself.
You are reading this book and it is also part of you, educating yourself and enriching you.

TAKE ALWAYS CALCULATED RISKS

People always say that you should not take risks, always follow a safe path, and always think of your family before doing that thing.

Definitely it is right but you cannot do anything without taking risk. Hence it is important to take CALCULATED RISK while you are going to do new things.

What does it mean? It means you should prepare a second alternative before going ahead. When it goes wrong, then you have a path to return back. You should have many passive incomes which give earning when you are sitting in the home. This reduces your risk and simply can take risk. Also, you are not required to leave your job when you want to do something new. You can do side by side with a job till you get confidence as safe.

There is no money made without a risk taken. Whether it's starting a business or investing in stocks, every avenue to making money requires some risk. In order to make money, you have to take a chance that a venture or idea you have will pan out. Therefore, it is important to think deeply and evaluate multiple possible outcomes before you decide that an investment is worth it.

GIVE BACK TO SOCIETY OR NEEDY

It is time to return back, and it is important to give back to the community. This leads back to the first point about adding value to the world around you. If you earn some money, give some back to a cause you believe in. This way, you are adding value to the world after having added value to yourself.

This is 100% truth that when you give something to someone, it always returns back to you with many folded interests on it. You believe it or not, but if you just observe, you will realize it.

Another benefit of giving to charity is that people perceive you as a better person when you give to causes, they care about.

<u>PASSIVE INCOME</u>

It involves multiple ways of earning along with main earning like salary. Passive earning goes on for which you do not require to work. This has proved that every successful rich person has more than 5 passive incomes. Hence to become rich, you need to have more and more passive income. Without this, you cannot think of becoming rich.

Following are the Passive Income generating source:

Gold

Publish Book on which you get royalties

Shares, Bond, Stocks

Joint Venture with Someone in Business

Real Estate earning

Social Media Earnings

Overall, you cannot become without your strong desire to become and your wholehearted commitment for hard work and smart management.

INTERVIEWS OF RENOWNED PERSONALITIES

Mr. Milind Deoskar, IRSS
Secretary,
Railway Board

He is a dedicated executive & professional in Railways, particularly in the Materials Management section. He is keen on the interest of his customers in his mind, and is ready to take progressive steps to help them get the right inputs at lowest costs. He strives to improve the processes well beyond the routine and written rules. He is a great proponent of IT in the professional and personal aspect of life.

He is a BE in Mechanical Engineering and IRSS officer of 1986 Batch. He is good at playing all sports, chess and likes to read self-help books.

Q - What do you think that students should focus on, to go ahead in their future?

A –
1. I think everyone should know about their strength and weakness.
2. They must know the available opportunities in the market.
3. Assist the potential of themselves.

They should follow discipline, training, courage and face the situation in life, once you combine all three things together then **NO ONE CAN STOP YOU FROM SUCCESS**.

Q - What do you think about the present scenario of changes in the IT sector & the available opportunity for the new generation?

A – I feel everybody should develop their expertise in IT rather than keeping shallow knowledge about the field, otherwise you will be out of the competition and market too!

Q - Sir, as you are working in railways at a very high level so what is your approach to improve Indian Railway system?

A – In this respect I feel we have the best benchmark available in the corporate sector which we are following to make Indian railway on the top, we are making Indian railway very safe, economical, comfortable. We need to utilize common sense and should never lose focus on our objective.

Q - What would be the guidelines for the candidates in their life to get success?

A – Involve all stakeholder while taking decisions in respective fields and take decisions which you like or which you think can do. **BE POSITIVE IN LIFE**!

As I always say, focus and objective should be very clear to achieve all the above benchmark.
- Go with Your Gut.
- Learn from Your Past Decisions.
- Tell Others About Your Decisions.
- Maintain a Flexible Approach.

Thank you.

Mr. Prabhakar S.
Ex-Directorate Finance
Maharashtra State Electricity Board

He is an Electrical Engineer who did 35 Years of service in the Power Sector, especially Power Distribution and worked as a Director (Projects), MSEDCL. Prior he took over as a new Chief Engineer of Maharashtra State Electricity Distribution Commission Limited (MSEDCL), Pune division. He started his career as a Junior Engineer at Nashik division in 1989. He did BE Electrical from Government College of Engineering, Aurangabad. He likes Yoga and walking.

Q - Could you please brief me about your background and education?

A – I come from Parbhani, one of the most backward areas from the State of Maharashtra. We were a poor joint family, from childhood I used to sleep on the lap of my illiterate grandmother, however she was knowing abundant mythological and ethnic stories. She used to tell me the stories from Ramayana, Mahabharat and other regular grandma stories. This actually led the foundation of ethical values.

My education started from class 5th. One of the schools had an inspection. They picked up non-school going boys, I was one of them. They used us as a dummy for showing a required attendance. They trained us as a dummy. During these days they found something in me and they just managed a dummy transfer certificate and admitted me directly in class 5th. Later done BE in 1981 and MBA-Finance.

Q - What do you think about the changing scenario in the job market?

A – There is a tough competition in both Private as well as the government jobs. They have a multilevel tough screening process. In this process they extract your actual knowledge level, attitude, confidence level, level of integrity and character. Hard work, knowledge and aptitude is the key to success.

Job scenario is continuously changing both in government as well as in the private sector. After the Corona epidemic there will be drastic changes in the job scenario. Fittest will survive in the changing scenario. Success lies in Knowledge, Hard work, innovation and creativity.

Q - Comment on fast money-making fad among youngsters than good education?

A – Fast money-making fad comes from habit of wrong lifestyle, inspired by movies and movie stars. Focus of youngsters is shifted from learning to racer bikes, smart phones, friends, tie day, rose day and so on. Classrooms are empty and coffee shops are houseful. Students need to focus on learning and adopt "simple living and high thinking". Ratan Tata, Narayana Murthy, Sudha Murthy, Sindhutai Sapkal, Bill Gates, Stev Jobs should be your real heroes.

Q - Today's youngsters are more inclined to social media. Comment please.

A – Officials, politicians, corporates etc are making very good use of social media in fulfilment of their political goals. Youngsters are not really making good use of social media for achieving their career goals. They are performing certain activities so as to post pictures on social media. For example, they are risking their life for taking selfies at dangerous locations. There are multiple educational videos on social media, they can make knowledge groups and have meaningful chat.

Q - What you can suggest for HR policy in the government sector?

A – All the HR policies need to have "Human factor" in it. You may induct zero delay and zero pendency in Employee claims. Training should be continuous activity and must cover all the employees in a defined period. Develop a feedback system which must include direct feedback. You also need to develop your own sources of feedback.

Q - Guidelines for children and their parents for career

A – Education is a continuous process, you need to continuously upgrade your knowledge, acquire new skills in your profession. You must have some hobbies such as singing, painting, trek, etc. Daily exercise and meditation for not less than one hour is a must. You must learn, 'Time Management' to find time for your family and hobbies without sacrificing your official responsibility.

a) For youngsters: Read autobiographies of successful personalities, literature, books written by prominent authors. You will definitely find your role model in some of these books. Knowledge from these books will form your own way of thinking, ethical values and principles to be strictly followed in life. Be humble, companionate, loving, caring, respect your parents and elders.
b) For parents: Your actions should not differ from what you teach them. children learn from your actions. If you shout at them and abuse them, one day you will get it in return. If people respect each other, children will respect them, on the other hand if you quarrel in their presence, consider you lost them. If you respect your old age person and take good care of them, you will get the same from your children.

Q - Your takeaway guidelines for all.

A – At the end, how much money and property you have is not important. You must earn following three things in life;

1. Minimum one Real Friend, with whom you can share all the secrets of your life, share all your emotions without hesitation and download all the stress you have. He helps you in crucial decision making in your life. If you have an additional opposite gender friend it will be advantageous.

2. One shoulder where you can rest your head and shed tears.

3. A house, other than your own house, where you can enter at any time without hesitation.

These three supports will be helpful in your stressful days and you will never feel depressed. Don't expect anything from others, don't be a taker but be a giver. Think what more you can give to your family, friends, society and the organization you work for. Donate some part of your earnings to the needy poor.

At the end, if your natural behaviour is honest, compassionate, humble and follow ethical values with good moral character and work hard with full devotion, you will always be happy and successful in life. If you do not have any of the above, read more books and autobiographies.

Mrs. Renu Sharma, IRPS
Principal Chief Personnel Officer
Central Railway

She is currently the Principal Chief Personnel Officer in Central Railway. She was the first lady DRM of Pune Railway Division, 1990- batch officer of the Indian Railways Personnel Service (IRPS). Earlier she has worked as the Chief Personnel Officer at Research Designs and Standards Organisation (RDSO), Lucknow and in various positions in the North Eastern Railway, Northern Railway, Eastern Railway. She did her Masters in Chemistry. She likes to sing classical songs, watching motivational movies and books.

Q - What do you like to say about your background which would motivate all?

A –I had a middle-class background but ever since I was a child, I always looked up to my parents, both were working in State Government. This propelled me to perceive myself as a working woman in the future. I've had my education in different cities of UP.

Q - What do you think about the changing scenario for the job market in the Government and Private sector?

A – As per my views since there is job security in government jobs, a large number of graduates still opt for the government sector. But it is a clear fact that the creamy layer of good students especially the ones passing out from IITs and IIMs opt for the private sector as they have better salary packages and good career prospects.

Q - What is your view about fast making money fad in young generations rather than good education? Is it ok?

A – The value of good education is much more than the value of making fast money because making fast money is generally through illegal ways, one requires education to differentiate between ethical and unethical. One should opt for steady growth and for that education is necessary.

Q - Please comment on social media in respect of youngsters.

A –Social Media platforms such as Facebook, Snapchat, Instagram, WhatsApp are a sheer waste of time and mostly spreading false information which sometimes becomes very disastrous for the society as a whole. It also proves to be of distraction for the youngsters. They also fall for illegal acts such as the recent boy's locker room and Jamtara incidents.

Q - In which direction should our youngsters should work for their future career?

A – Youngsters should follow careers which suit their competence rather than conventional ones.

People generally overlook the academic merit of an individual and start analysing his talents but I think that academic excellence is equally important. Parents should not assume their roles to be just as a drag but act as facilitator in shaping the career of their children.

For job satisfaction, it is very important that they should understand the challenges and the significance attached to their posts. They should try to grab opportunities for decision making and creativity during day to day working.

It is also important to be tactful in a positive manner in dealing with the superiors as well as the juniors for self-satisfaction. Time management and organised way of working is important.

Last but not the least it is very important to plan short term and long-term self-made goals and try to achieve them within time. This gives maximum job satisfaction.

Q - What would be guidelines for our parents for their children?

A – Parents should not pressurize their children in the fields in which they are not interested. Besides studies, children should also be motivated to follow some extracurricular activities which help in building the overall personality which is very important for job and interviews, be it private or government sector. Parents should promote their children to be frank with them and there should always be an atmosphere of open dialogue between the parents and their children so that the best decisions can be taken while deciding the career.

Q - What do you like to give a take away point for all?

A – The most important things which I would like to highlight on the issue are:
- The parents should act as guiding factors rather than compulsively forcing their children towards the career of their choice. · Class and college merits are equally important as are the extra-curricular activities.
- The career planning should not be done based just upon the present socio-economic scenarios but should be based on very specific analysis of the future market.

As per my view the thing of paramount importance is self-actualisation and happiness. All other worldly things like money, career, job satisfaction is secondary to it.

Mr. Manoj Pande, IRPS
Member Staff, Ex-Officio Secretary
Government of India, Delhi

He is an Indian Railways Personnel Service IRPS of 1981 Batch has taken over as Member Staff, Railway Board and Ex - Officio Secretary to Government of India on 2nd November,19. Prior he was working as Director General, Personnel Railway Board. He has worked in various capacities in different Railways beginning with Central Railway and in Diesel Locomotive Works, Western Railway, West Central Railway, South Central Railway and South Eastern Railway. He was the Principal Chief Personnel Officer for over 12 years. He has an interest in Railway Heritage, its history where he wrote many books. He did PG in Economics, LLB, MBA (HR) and knows Russian language. He likes to read motivational books and current affairs.

Q - What do you like to say about your background which would motivate all of us?

A –Being born in Delhi and having studied in a good school as well as a good college, I will not say that I come from a deprived background. But this did not make me feel superior. I clearly understood very early that I have to plan my studies for any competitive examination, where persons from all kinds of backgrounds appear. Therefore, in order to succeed I had to expand my horizons and knowledge beyond my subject of study in college, which was economics.

Reading became a habit. Newspapers, magazines, novels, non-fiction all expanded my thinking and have kept me aware of what is going around us. It helped me clear the Civil Services exam in the first attempt without any coaching or any help book for competitive examinations. This interest in reading continues even today.

Q - What do you think about the changing scenario for the job market in the Government and Private sector?

A – In the early 1980s when I was to enter the job market, the opportunities in India for someone who was not an engineer or a doctor, were either in Government, Banking or in teaching. Private sector jobs were very few. All this changed after liberalization of the economy in the 1990s as well-paid jobs increased in the private sector. Besides the traditional jobs in government, banking and law there are opportunities growing in the IT field, mass media, NGOs and even education.

There are also opportunities in e-commerce also especially in the smaller towns and self-employment in niche areas should grow. Start-Ups are actively encouraged, and many young entrepreneurs have changed from being job seekers to being job providers like FlipKart, OYO Rooms, OLA, Zomato, etc..

Q - Comment on fast money-making fad among youngsters than good education?

A – One must never forget the adage "easy come, easy go". Unless there is basic background, one may not achieve the desired goals and initial fast money may vanish quickly. Remember, cardboard plywood does not last as much as teakwood furniture. An average working career is more than 30 years. One will have to learn new things and compete with others in this period. Even if quick money has been earned initially, such earnings have also to be sustained in the long run. Therefore, good education is essential as it provides a solid base. And not only good education, one must keep on learning new things and keep abreast of technology. Short term courses and training are essential. Experience alone is not enough as it may cease to be relevant 10-15 years later.

Q - As a higher authority in the HR field in Indian Railways, what are the focus areas to improve HR of Indian Railways?

A – Indian Railways, despite getting better technology continues to be labour intensive as a result of which staff expenditure constitutes substantial part of costs. It cannot be the case that we spend both on high-cost technology yet do not productively utilize the available manpower. Moreover, some activities which can be outsourced and done in a better manner continue to be done in-house.

So, the focus has to be on improving staff productivity by multi-skilling, review of redundant activities, and identification of surpluses, incentivizing training and providing accelerated promotional avenues to the more skilled staff. It is our effort to meet staff requirements for new activities, in-house by way of Vacancy Bank. In addition, areas where reviews can lead to more productivity (e.g. Train Crew Running Links) will be essential. This requires a proactive approach by all, not merely the HR department. Staff Welfare has been and should remain a focus area as it makes Indian Railways a better choice for the future entrants to the workforce.

Q - In which direction should our youngsters should work for their future career?

A – Ideally, a young person of today should be a self-employed person. If employed, choose a career that will be professionally satisfying and monetarily also rewarding. It has to be commensurate either with your educational background or your interest.

And remember, youth shall not last forever. So, pay adequate attention to exercise and have healthy eating habits. As stress will always be there, have some hobbies or develop some interest that takes your mind away, even if for a very short period, from the causes of stress. This is absolutely essential.

Q - What would be guidelines for our youngsters and parents for their children?

A – A good part of your day and a major portion of your adult life are spent on your work. It could be a job where you work for someone else or self-employed. The objective has to be to excel in whatever you do. Even if the initial job is not to your liking, you should not give up. Set yourself a higher goal & work consciously to achieve it. There are hundreds and hundreds of examples where people rise in life due to hard work.

Late Dhirubhai Ambani worked in a petrol station in Aden and later came back to India and founded Reliance, which is the 321 biggest companies in India today. Hundreds start in low paid jobs and rise to become Civil Servants and Managers. It is all due to confidence, calibre and hard work. Do not attribute everything to bad luck. At least try. Even if you do not succeed, you would gain valuable learning's for the future.

At the end, the journey of life should be enjoyed. Plan and work to achieve personal and professional goals, never neglecting good health.

Mr. Shrikant Deshpande, IAS
Chief Electoral Officer,
Additional Chief Secretary,
Government of Maharashtra

He is from village Diskal in Satara district, took his education up to 7th class from there and later up to 12th science from Deccan Education Society, Satara. He did his B.Tech from University Department of Chemical Technology (UDCT) MUMBAI. Later he did M.Tech from IIT Madras. After that, he joined a private company in 1987 and Bharati Vidyapeeth for doing UPSC preparation in 1988.

He cleared UPSC by 40th rank in 1991 with PHYSICS AND MATHS. Best part is that he got the highest mark in both subjects in India - 450 in each which shows his talent. Shri Deshpande focuses that during preparation you need to have good friends, reading habits and keep moral high during it.

Q - What do you think about the changing scenario in the education sector? Also comment on the changing job market with COVID impact.

A –Classroom culture is going to change and it is an opportunity for all. As per situation, everybody should change. Now remote location working would be a normal phenomenon whereas urbanization reduces with villages will grow. Online industry and internet will grow.

Q - Now social media is growing in a faster way. What do you think about a career in these areas for youngsters with education?

A – It is already in the system but in COVID it is seen in a larger way. Otherwise, youngsters are getting attracted to this and trying to make a career in this. No doubt any one can think in this, but need to do a career with proper education and backup due to huge volatility in this sector.

Q - Being an IAS and working on United Nations assignment in Africa, you are doing excellent work and ideal figure for all, what would you like to guide youngsters for opportunities in UNITED NATIONS, WORLD BANK and others? Please guide how to prepare for this?

A – People and youngsters do not know about international opportunities. During graduation or PG who are abroad or in India, they should apply for internship in these organizations. Once you get in, you will learn how it works and how you should prepare for the YOUNG PROFESSIONAL PROGRAM in which you can get selected through INTERNATIONAL CIVIL SERVICE COMMISSION (ICSC).

Each organization like the World Health Organization (WHO), ILO, UN, UNDP etc have their own YPP which is administered by the ICSC. It is like Indian Civil Service Exam where officers are recruited in IAS, IFS, IPS, IRPS, IRS etc. Author has given all details; you can see in this book.

For professional-DEPUTATION, those who are working in government or private, also they can apply with an expert field with their experience for short tenure like 1 to 4 years. It is a very satisfying experience with good job and financial benefits. Choose a field, apply on the HR gateway of the UN or respective portal. You will succeed.

Q - What would be your guidelines for youngsters and parents for their children in regard to their future career?

A – First, support you or your child where you like to work from the core of your heart. If you like the work, then you enjoy work and excel in life. Hence let the youngsters do work where they want. Just guide and support them with your supervision.

Youngsters have great international opportunities for all in India and abroad, apply in it in various fields like finance, supply chain management, programming, administration etc.

Q - Please kindly share your best moments in life or career.

A – CEO, Raigad District- During this time, personally worked for demarcated lands to Tribal Peoples where there was a lot of conflict. After this, they started to get benefits from the government scheme. It was a satisfying experience.

Afghanistan, during this tenure, developed Administrative Reform for Government policy. Now it is a role model for the Afghanistan Government. South Sudan- Presently working here where a lot of communal conflicts used to happen. In this, innovative ideas were implemented and worked with people which leads to reduced violence. Hence people see with respect and gratitude.

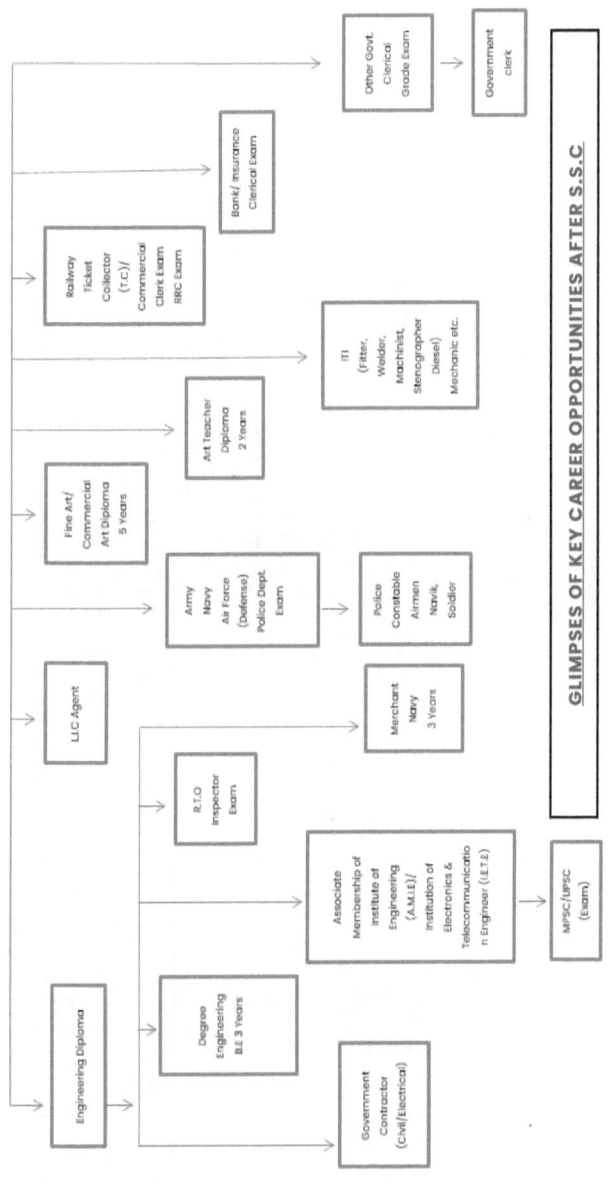

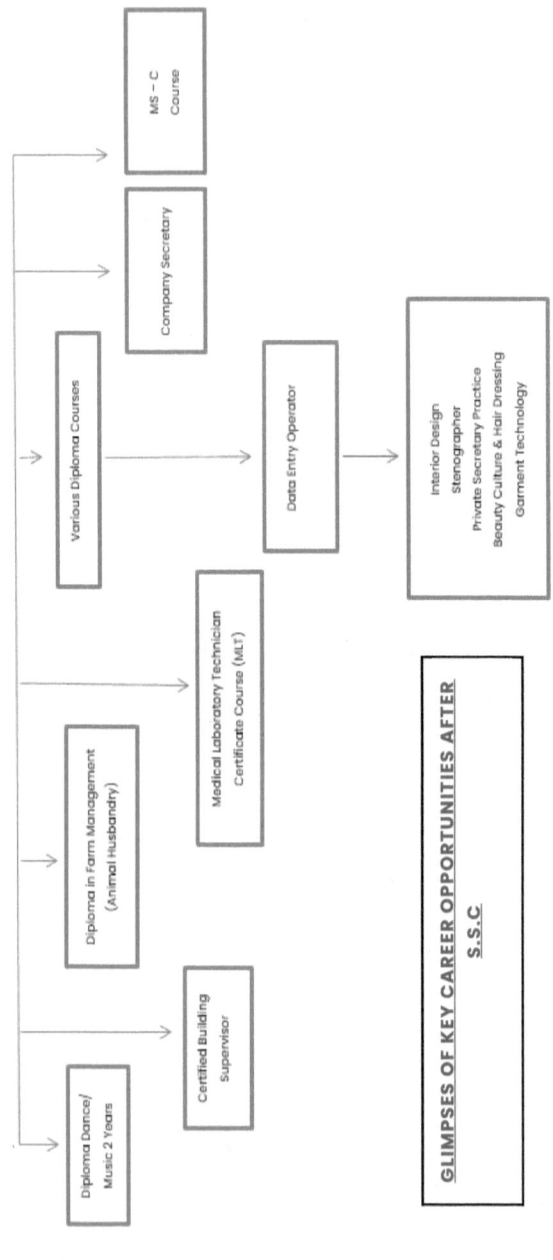

GLIMPSES OF KEY CAREER OPPORTUNITIES AFTER H.S.C

IF CHOOSING COMMERCE:

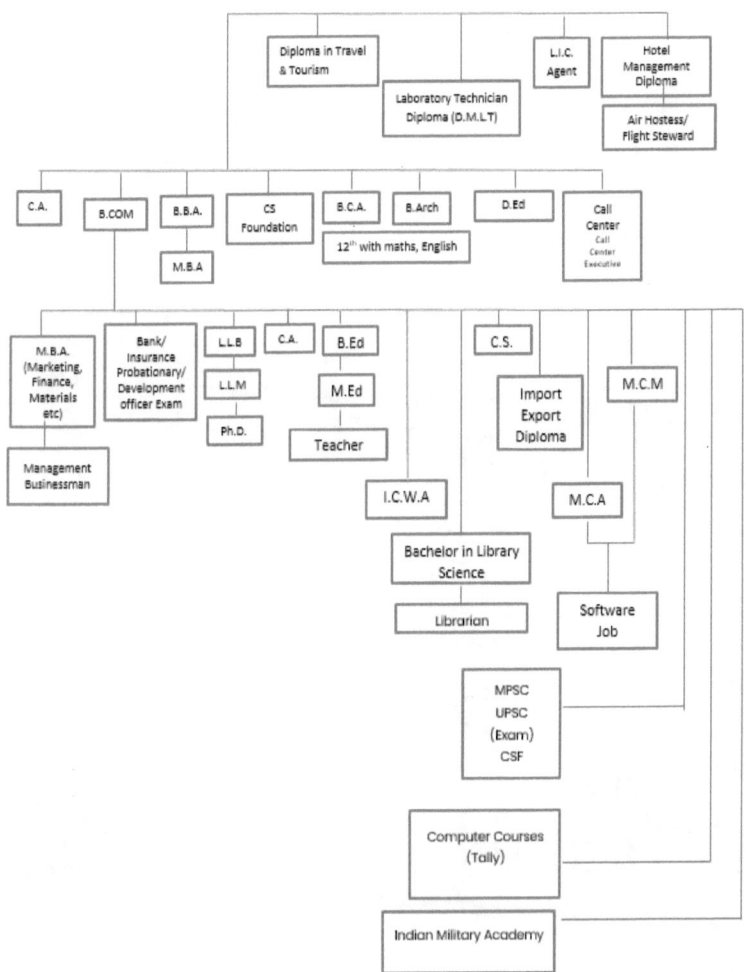

GLIMPSES OF KEY CAREER OPPORTUNITIES AFTER H.S.C

IF CHOOSING ARTS:

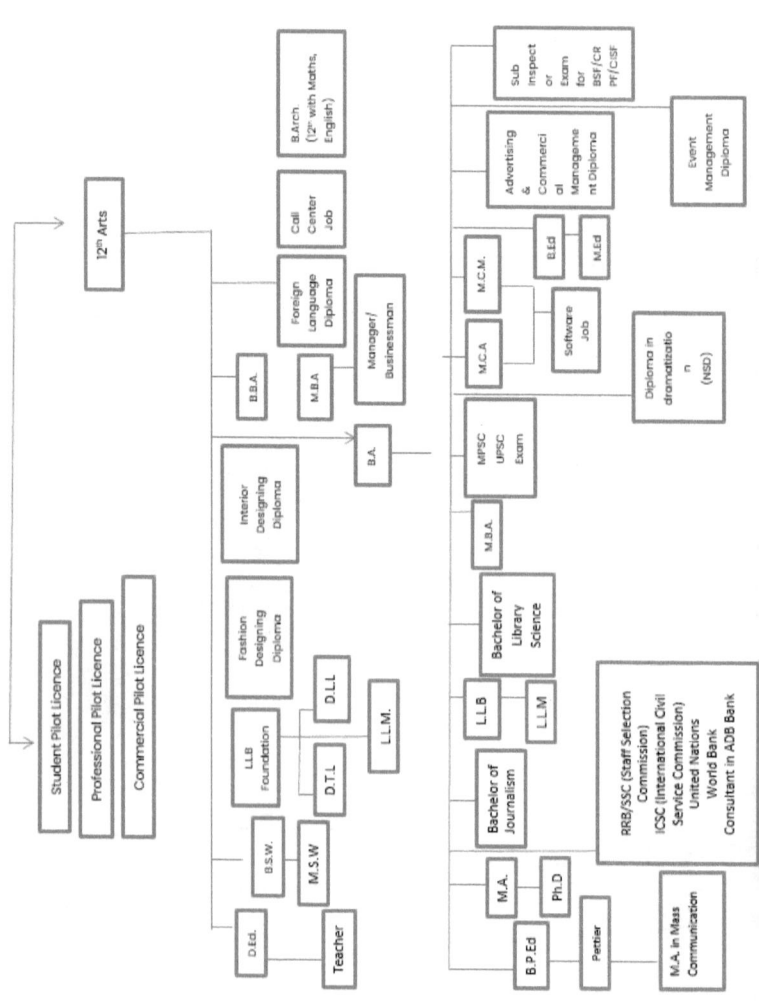

GLIMPSES OF KEY CAREER OPPORTUNITIES AFTER H.S.C

IF CHOOSING SCIENCE WITH PCMB:

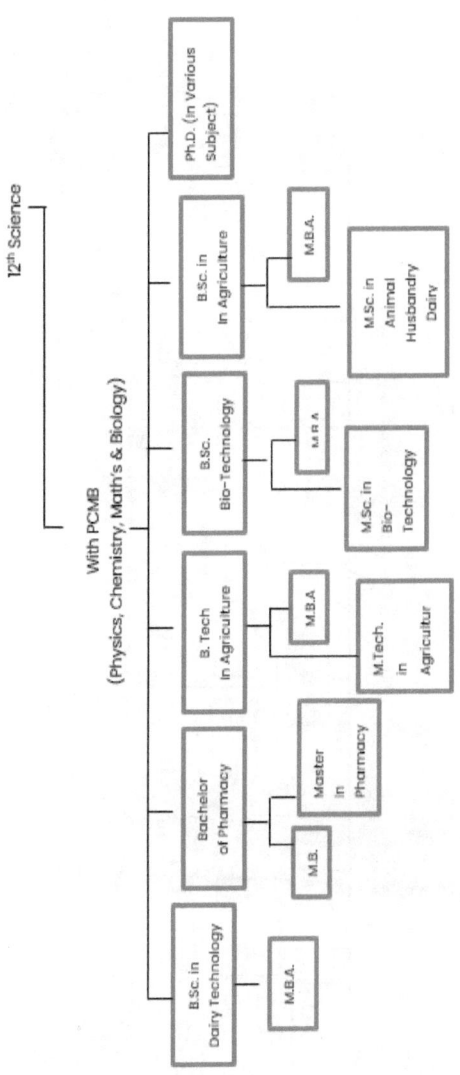

GLIMPSES OF KEY CAREER OPPORTUNITIES AFTER H.S.C

IF CHOOSING SCIENCE WITH PCB:

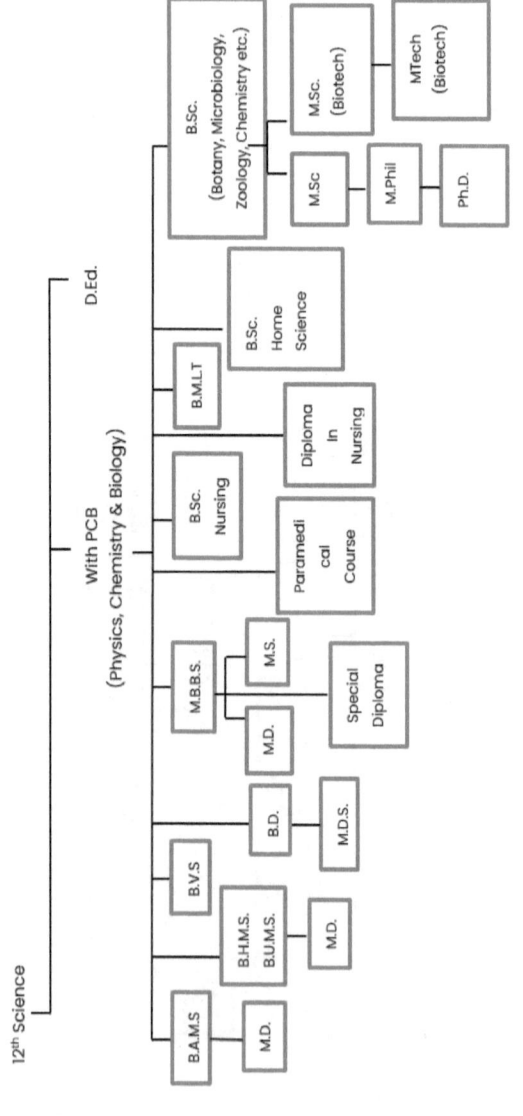

GLIMPSES OF KEY CAREER OPPORTUNITIES AFTER H.S.C

IF CHOOSING SCIENCE WITH PCM:

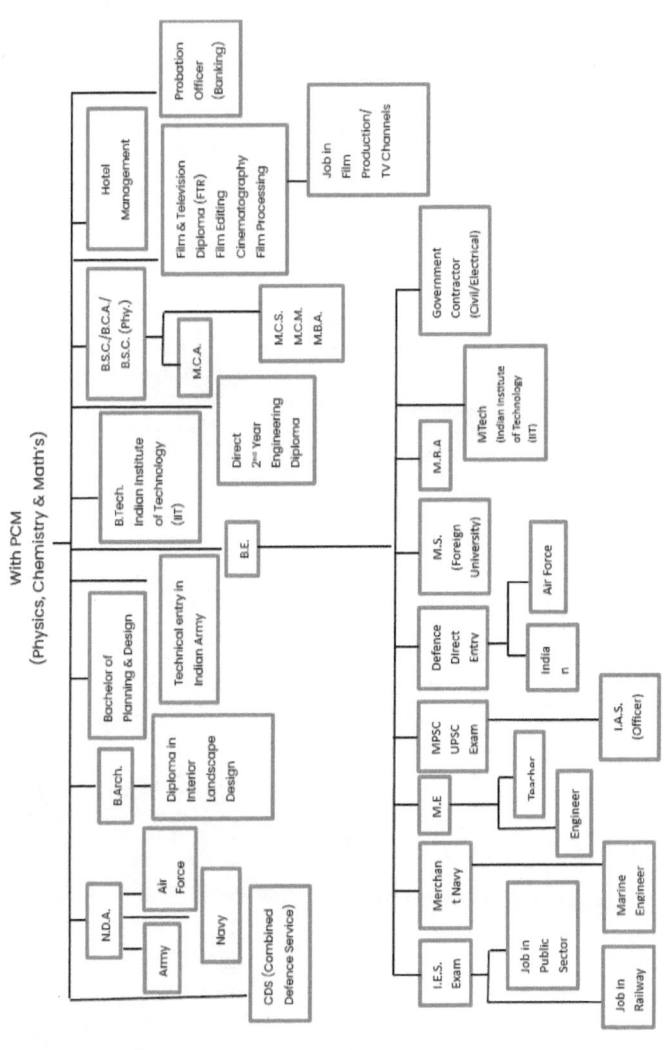

www.ingramcontent.com/pod-product-compliance
Lightning Source LLC
LaVergne TN
LVHW041710070526
838199LV00045B/1287